Developing a Trauma-Informed
Perspective in School Communities

Developing a Trauma-Informed Perspective in School Communities

An Introduction for Educators, School Counselors, and Administrators

Lynn Heramis

cognella®
SAN DIEGO

Bassim Hamadeh, CEO and Publisher
Amy Smith, Project Editor
Emely Villavicencio, Senior Graphic Designer
Stephanie Kohl, Licensing Associate
Natalie Piccotti, Director of Marketing
Kassie Graves, Vice President of Editorial
Jamie Giganti, Director of Academic Publishing

Cover image copyright © 2019 iStockphoto LP/wildpixel.

9781516579334

3970 Sorrento Valley Blvd., Ste. 500, San Diego, CA 92121

Brief Contents

Detailed Contents

Preface

M ANY ELEMENTARY AND secondary classroom teachers, administrators, and other school personnel have an untapped power of maintaining a position to create formative and positive change in schools, yet they may often be unaware of the possibilities to provide essential healing experiences that can help support students struggling with potentially traumatic experiences. *Developing a Trauma-Informed Perspective for School Communities: An Introduction for Educators, School Counselors, and Administrators* is a supplemental introductory text that will help inform future and current school counselors, educators, and leadership teams about some of the latest research on several topics necessary for developing a trauma-informed perspective. Some of these topics include attachment, neuroscience, adverse childhood experiences (ACEs), toxic stress, mindfulness, self-care, and resiliency. A foundation of basic knowledge and awareness of these topics will aid in developing a shift toward having the mindset and skills to recognize how signs of potential trauma may appear and how to best support individuals exhibiting such behaviors through a whole-school approach. This text is not meant to provide a step-by-step implementation process, as true trauma-informed practices maintain a flexible framework that requires purposeful planning and staff collaboration initiated by a leadership team within a school staff or district. The goal of this book is to plant the seeds for priming educators' brains for what is to come in this exciting time of brain and trauma research as the urgency of this topic continues to lead to its introduction into schools across the country and abroad.

Professional development training for teachers often discusses how important it is to meet students where they are in order to be successful and not where we expect them to be without considering a lack of earlier basic foundational support. With the significant research that continues to evolve regarding childhood trauma, attachment, neuroscience, and interpersonal neurobiology, the time has come for us to meet educators and school support staff where *they are* in order to give them the tools they need to feel passionate about their work and serve confidently in their roles. This includes building educator capacity for trauma-informed practices and allowing educators to experience cultivation of relationships themselves if they have not been afforded earlier opportunities. In order to meet the needs of the *whole child*, we must also support the *whole educator,* given that a wealth of research confirms how relationships and social-emotional development are essential components to children's learning processes.

Students spend a considerable amount of time in school with educators annually, providing the space and time for adults to build meaningful relationships and foster a sense of safety while modeling healthy styles of interaction that may not exist in the majority of a student's life. When we are not aware of what triggers our own distress during the school day and we do not invest in our own self-care to know how to maintain our composure in the presence of students with trauma histories and difficult behaviors, where will our students find the modeling they may desperately need to be successful with academic, social, and emotional development? Developing a trauma-informed perspective allows us to disrupt the patterns potentially preventing educators from demonstrating true empathy and compassion with students who may be struggling with trauma through difficult behaviors. Because trauma-informed approaches require a refining of practices over time, ongoing reflection, and investment in working on the self as an educator, setbacks in the process are expected and necessary for practicing positive shifts in ways of being and supportive professional relationships. We cannot expect our students to learn from their mistakes and thrive if we are not able to model our own wellness and empowerment in readiness for the unexpected, unknown, or discomfort with life challenges.

Purpose and Structure of the Book

This book's purpose is to provide a foundation of knowledge related to the science and research fueling the apparent need for trauma-informed practices in schools, which has typically not been included in the curriculum for education programs preparing school counselors and other leaders in the field of education (Goodman-Scott, 2015; O'Grady, 2017). There is an urgency to address the increasing need for schools to respond to and support various types of student issues stemming from potential trauma, as school staff members frequently encounter student behaviors or situations they do not feel confidently equipped to support. A challenge that consistently arises when advocating for students during consultations with educators is the robust skepticism toward accepting the paradigm shift from an often ineffective deficit mindset of quick "fixing" to a holistic and collective approach that requires patience while addressing student behaviors through relationships to encourage development of self-efficacy skills. The extreme difficulty getting buy-in from current school staff about trauma-informed approaches that is still so common and strong throughout many educational climates confirms the dire need for its introduction in education training programs. Understanding how relationships play a crucial role in healing trauma and building strong communities ultimately impacts school attitudes and creates a paradigm shift toward authentic safety and security (Cozolino, 2013; Perry, 2017; Siegel, 2015).

The text includes a restatement of research not easily accessible or acknowledged in introductory courses yet significantly relevant to the study of any field related to working with students in a school environment. Each chapter contains a brief "Self-Check" and a brief "Reflection" question related to the section it follows, which allows readers to engage in reflecting about how their past experiences might be impacting their current practices with students. Each chapter also concludes with one or more "Practice" exercises and one "Connect and Reflect" section that apply the concepts from the chapter to real-world situations, includes critical thinking questions, and additionally explores how the reader might approach specific situations considering best practices. Chapters 2, 3, and 6 provide links to brief videos to supplement the reader's learning of the chapter's content. A case study is also included at the end of each chapter to provide context for the chapter's topic in a school scenario with discussion questions. A majority of these features require much reflection by the reader, which is necessary for enhancing skills in developing educator capacity for providing trauma-informed approaches with students.

Benefits of the Book

My own sense of personal success in my work with students and colleagues develops from the internal gratification that is felt from making an intentional effort to reflect on valuable past experiences and apply research-based neuroscientific principles to the art of human relationships. What that looks like exactly cannot be described in a fixed manner, nor can it develop overnight, as it transpires from each individual's way of being with others that embodies an authentic lifelong practice of understanding the primary value of meaningful relationships in fostering positive neural development. What it *can* do is help the healing processes for individuals struggling with trauma through shared restorative moments of being fully present, engaged and connected. It is an energy you might feel when you walk into a school building based on your interactions with multiple students and staff that gives you a sense of safety, inclusion, trust, camaraderie, and inspiration to be your best self. It is not enough for just one or a few staff members in a school building to understand the impacts of trauma on students, as buffering healing environments are only strengthened by consistency within a collective team of professionals committed to investing in the current and future well-being of students, families, educational systems, and communities.

Schools have a collective responsibility to meet student needs, and developing awareness about the impacts of trauma through reflection processes is the first step toward creating a responsive and holistic model that embraces connection and integrates trauma-informed education. An additional benefit that comes with successful experiences and outcomes over time is that this process fosters a desire to seek out additional learning to enhance professional knowledge and practices about supporting students using universal approaches. This text provides a basic overview of related disciplines contributing to the latest relevant research on brain and human development in order to stay current in the field and empower professionals to step into the education field with a basis of knowledge that will enhance their skills and practice with students. It also discusses common terms associated with trauma-informed care for undergraduate and graduate students who are preparing to enter a field they passionately and profoundly aspire to serve and, as anyone who has worked in elementary and secondary education can attest, are typically at extremely high risk for burnout. Undergraduate and graduate students can intentionally apply this awareness to their continuing studies and future work in schools and communities to advocate for meaningful and systemic change toward a whole-school trauma-informed approach.

Chapter 1

The Need for Trauma-Informed Schools

W HAT THOUGHTS IMMEDIATELY come to mind when you hear the word *trauma*? Maybe you think about physical abuse, neglect, or assault. Or it could be that you envision specific incidents such as a school shooting, a fatal car accident, the death of a loved one, a kidnapping, or a terrorist attack. Any of these examples have the potential for creating traumatic experiences, which can unfortunately result in negative physical and emotional responses beyond an individual's control. Trauma has the power of seeping into our everyday lives in the most intricate and subtle ways. A common view of trauma has often been related to a catastrophic event, a natural disaster, or an acute crisis.

Schools have a collective responsibility to meet the challenging needs of students struggling with trauma by creating a physically and emotionally safe learning environment. It is important to understand the harmful impacts of punitive discipline for students in schools, especially when their negative behaviors can potentially stem from responses to traumas that are not recognized by educators and support staff. This specific need for providing a positive, responsive, and holistic school community as a means for healing and reducing trauma-related behaviors can be met by first equipping educators with basic knowledge about trauma, trauma-informed mindsets, and the understanding that there is meaning behind behavior.

Current research indicates the foundation of trauma encompasses a wider range of sources than previously acknowledged. One of the most enlightening discoveries from the last decade of research holds great significance for our work in schools: our patterns of experiences related to daily human interactions can either help exacerbate

Learning Objectives

1. What are the history and rationale driving schools toward trauma-informed approaches?

2. What is *trauma,* and what does it mean to be *trauma-informed*?

3. What are the four key assumptions of a trauma-informed approach described by the Substance Abuse and Mental Health Services Administration?

4. What are the basic differences between trauma-informed and non-trauma-informed mindsets?

or help heal the body's response systems to trauma, ultimately affecting the course of how we function for the rest of our lives. Unresolved trauma has the capacity to develop into serious issues that become difficult for an individual to heal from when the body is involuntarily wired for survival in response to constant states of stress or fear. This discovery creates the potential capacity for school environments to become increasingly challenging for school counselors, teachers, administrators, and additional school staff to support and maintain an appropriate level of wellness.

This chapter will begin with an introduction to the recent history of school practices in public education that continue to support the current desire for trauma-informed approaches in schools and will continue with a basic approach to recognizing the difference between a trauma-informed and non-trauma-informed mindset to help develop an understanding of how authentic human connection, trust, and respect are at the core of a positive relational culture.

> ### Reflection
>
> What are some reasons you are choosing to join the education field and work in school settings?

Zero Tolerance Policies

The widely accepted zero tolerance school practices regarding discipline measures over the past two decades in the United States has progressed into a culture of imposing severe and unjust consequences across educational settings, particularly for disadvantaged youth and students of color (Heitzeg, 2009). Unfortunate occurrences of school shootings and gun violence in U.S. schools during the late 1980s and 1990s sparked national concern over safety in schools and resulted in Congress passing the Gun-Free Schools Act of 1994, requiring states to mandate expulsion of students for possession of firearms on school property. This led to the adoption of zero tolerance policies across the nation and developed into a prevalent reliance on suspension or expulsion to address student issues beyond the initial intention of creating such policies, such as disruptive classroom behavior.

Zero tolerance policies initially served as a resolution to address student possession and/or use of firearms, weapons, alcohol, and drugs on school property. Although the intention of such harmful and punitive policies was meant to maintain a safe and secure learning environment, these counterproductive practices evolved into negative outcomes that continue to push students out of school by means of expulsion, suspension, and arrests for nonviolent or slight violations of student conduct policies (Heitzeg, 2009). This ultimately contributes to what is known as the *school-to-prison pipeline*, a system in which public schools have served as "feeder" schools for the criminal justice system by enforcing extreme disciplinary action through suspension/expulsion *and* referrals to the juvenile justice system (Advancement Project, 2005). Such school policies used as a "one-size-fits-all" response to address intentional misbehavior of students also apply severe punishments to student behavior related to emotional issues or other disabilities, thus neglecting to acknowledge or understand the circumstances of misbehavior or any potential influence of a student's particularly unique experiences leading up to the misconduct (American Bar Association, 2001). Additionally, youth minorities are disproportionately affected by the excessive and unnecessary involvement with the justice system due to the focus on offenses rather than student needs (Justice Policy Institute, 2018). Consequences such as out-of-school suspension may lead youth to engage in criminal behavior, predominantly the African American population in comparison to Caucasian youth (Cuellar & Markowitz, 2015).

Several documented incidents demonstrate how zero tolerance policies have been used as inappropriate responses to student behaviors labeled as defiant and disrespectful, resulting in life-changing unintended consequences for affected students (National Child Traumatic Stress Network, 2017). Numerous school incidents have been reported over the last two decades that are related to unjust punishments. Following are just a few examples, documented in the research from the Advancement Project (2005), of specific cases in which students were given consequences leading to suspension or expulsion that may have accompanied unnecessary referrals into the juvenile or criminal justice systems due to the implementation of zero tolerance policies:

- A 10-year old elementary student was pulled out of class and hand-cuffed for bringing an 8-inch pair of scissors to school and was held at the police station for 8 hours. Scissors were included in the state law's definition of a potential weapon. The student was not charged, since it was clear that the student was using the scissors for a school project and had no intentions of using them as a weapon but was still suspended for 5 days.
- A high school student in North Carolina was criminally charged and potentially faced 30 days in jail for cursing in front of a teacher. Charges were dropped.
- An 8-year-old student in Kentucky hit and kicked his teacher as she attempted to physically remove him from the classroom for misbehaving. The student was charged with felony assault, although the juvenile court judge ultimately dismissed the charges.

Reflection

What are some of your initial thoughts about or reactions to these examples? Discuss whether you agree or disagree with any of the consequences given for each student in each example and explain why.

Since these harsh disciplinary measures have frequently been used in response to minor or nonviolent infractions, zero tolerance policies do not take into consideration the lack of differentiation between students with intent to harm and students with behavioral issues that require mental and emotional support (American Bar Association, 2001). The unfortunate outcomes for many vulnerable and behaviorally challenged students include unnecessary emotional trauma, embarrassment, denial of education from forced absence in the classroom, and inaccurate stigma and labeling as "delinquents" or "criminals" (Heitzeg, 2009; Sporleder & Forbes, 2016).

SELF-CHECK

Reflect on what you feel your strengths are as an educator or school specialist. What areas might you need growth in and why? Try to include areas of academics, your attitude(s) toward education, and your relationships with students.

Trauma-Informed Schools in Action

Lincoln High, an alternative high school located in the rural city of Walla Walla, Washington, was widely known by the community as one of the most underperforming schools in the district due to its consistently chaotic environment. Students at Lincoln High were transferred from the main high school in Walla Walla, which led to several challenges for Lincoln High's faculty and staff, who were dealing with a wide array of serious student issues, such as substance abuse, low academic achievement, truancy, arrests, and physical fights (Pritzker, Scully, & Redford, 2015).

Jim Sporleder joined the faculty as the new principal of Lincoln High and initially experienced a school climate that was desperately out of control and ineffective in using traditional methods of addressing student behaviors. Sporleder attended a conference in 2010 regarding complex trauma, where he learned about the Adverse Childhood Experiences (ACE) study and the significant impacts of neglect and abuse on the neural and physical development of children. The evidence presented in the ACE study sparked Sporleder's motivation for creating successful change in approaches with students as a school, ultimately transforming Lincoln High into an environment where students are able to thrive with the unconditional support and guidance of the adults they encounter every single day at school.

The results were dramatically astounding, as disciplinary office referrals decreased from 600 in 2009–2010 to 320 in 2010–2011 and then continued to decline to 280 referrals in 2011–2012 and 242 in 2012–2013 (Sporleder & Forbes, 2016). Additional positive outcomes were measured, such as significant decreases in school incidents involving police and the total number of days students were not present in school as well as increases in graduation rates and state assessment scores (Sporleder & Forbes, 2016). This remarkable achievement gained warranted widespread recognition, which led to the filming of Lincoln High in the documentary *Paper Tigers* during the 2012–2013 school year. The term "trauma-informed" in reference to schools was coined as the new cutting-edge approach to addressing the impacts of trauma that can create barriers to student learning as well as student behaviors that challenged the zero tolerance policies that had become widely accepted and normalized as the default method for discipline in schools. Other schools and districts in Washington state followed suit and began implementing trauma-informed practices under this model, and training on trauma-informed approaches is increasingly becoming highly desired or required for school staff in various districts/schools across the country. In some cases, outsourced professionals are required to have trauma-informed training before stepping into school buildings as support staff so that students struggling with trauma histories can be appropriately supported and unintended retraumatization does not occur. Lincoln High is an example of an extremely high-needs student population. Other school populations vary, as every school culture is unique to its surrounding community.

During the 2014–2015 school year, Park Middle School in Antioch, California, had reached a student suspension rate of 19.2 percent by the month of February (Udesky, 2018). Repeated suspensions did not have positive impacts on disruptive student behavior, and teachers were becoming discouraged, on the verge of burnout. The school initiated a 3-year trauma-informed program to shift from a toxic organization with low morale to a healthy culture that fosters resilience and healthy relationships for students. After only 2 years of incorporating this program, the rate of suspensions remarkably decreased to 8.4 percent, more than a 50 percent drop (Udesky, 2018).

Many of the issues currently facing education include systems that are not equipped with enough resources to support the wide array of student needs, especially when the students come to school with unique experiences influencing various levels of social, emotional, and cognitive abilities and challenges (Cozolino, 2014). Children who often come to school feeling tired, hungry, distressed, and isolated from exposure to a wide array of issues—such as homelessness, incarceration, alcohol, drugs, neglect, abuse, or mental health issues—are often deprived of meaningful connections with family, school, and community and are at risk for failing out of school or struggling with learning challenges (Wolpow, Johnson, Hertel, & Kincaid, 2016). With the emerging research in the fields of neuroscience, attachment and interpersonal neurobiology, understanding trauma and its devastating impacts on student learning and mental/ physical health is beneficial and necessary for supporting the diverse needs of school populations. As a result, compassionate relationships and authentic nurturing experiences offered to students may serve as a gateway to reversing the damaging effects of trauma.

Introduction to Trauma

According to the Substance Abuse and Mental Health Services Administration (SAMHSA), "Individual trauma results from an **event**, series of events, or set of circumstances that is **experienced** by an individual as physically or emotionally harmful or life threatening and that has lasting adverse **effects** on the individual's functioning and mental, physical, social, emotional, or spiritual well-being" (SAMHSA, 2014, p. 7). SAMHSA focuses on the three *E*s of trauma that are all mentioned in the above definition: *events*, *experience*, and *effects*.

Events in this description may translate into a single or repeated occurrence and encompasses severe threat or neglect that endangers healthy development, and adverse *effects* characterized as prolonged may either occur immediately or be delayed. *Experiences* involve each individual's unique perception of what has happened that may or may not result in trauma with physical and emotional responses. For example, any event may be experienced as traumatic for one child and not for another, and this is determined by how an individual interprets and applies meaning to a particular event; "responses to these experiences often manifest in behaviors or conditions that result in involvement with the child welfare and the criminal and juvenile justice system or in difficulties in the education, employment, or primary care system" (SAMHSA, 2014, p. 5).

Trauma has also been defined in various ways as it specifically relates to the school setting. Wolpow, Johnson, Hertel, and Kincaid (2016) describe trauma as "an umbrella term denoting the inability of an individual or community to respond in a healthy way (physically, emotionally, and/or mentally) to acute or chronic stress. Trauma occurs when stress compromises the health and welfare of a person and his/her community" (p. xiv). This definition of trauma focuses on an individual's overwhelming stress levels as a result of experiencing an event and the individual's unhealthy responses as a result of such stress.

A wide range of experiences have the potential to cause trauma to a child, and the behavior or anxiety manifesting from such trauma is often met with judgement or dismissive remarks by an observer who may not understand the context of the situation. As a result, thoughts or statements from an adult uninformed about trauma may include the following, which assume an impression that may exhibit an unwillingness to be receptive or understanding about another individual's experience(s). As you read them, consider that they could be addressed to a child who has not yet reached cognitive, emotional, or physical maturity appropriate for their developmental level:

1. It's not a big deal
2. You're choosing to act this way
3. Just get over it
4. You need to get tough
5. You're fine
6. I got through it, and I'm fine

Just as with zero tolerance policies, identifying traumatic experiences is not a "one-size-fits-all" classification, nor should it be used in that manner regarding school discipline policies.

We will expand further with more depth on trauma and how it impacts our neurobiology in Chapters 2 and 3 and explore how the type of responses above can relationally cause significant harm to a child's healing process when their behavior is a symptom of trauma. To begin the process of developing a trauma-informed perspective, it is essential to broaden our personal views of which experiences can potentially generate trauma and look beyond our own biases to make sure we are not causing continued harm to a child who is depending on us for safety and healing. Romero, Robertson, and Warner (2018) explain that:

> Educators may also have in-group biases and can be more critical towards someone who looks like them or had similar childhoods than someone not in that group (e.g., teachers who grew up poor and now teach poor students, White teachers assuming all staff of color grew up poor and vice versa). It's the *I made it; what's wrong with you?* And not the *I made it and I want to help you too.* If you find yourself having in-group bias, stop and do some deep self-analysis and work toward seeing yourself at the same age as your student and what you would have wanted a teacher or principal to see in you. A student whose daily home life is full of adversity not only needs you as a role model but needs you to help feed his or her resiliency. (p. 58)

What is the general overarching goal of schools? If it is to provide a physically and emotionally safe and equitable learning environment that supports the academic success of all students, then it is necessary for schools to take into consideration the unique experiences of each student as they enter school each day and be sensitive to how those experiences can positively or negatively impact their ability to learn, as well as how a school and classroom climate contribute to a student's ability to achieve academic success. The inverted-U learning curve developed by Yerkes and Dodson (1908) demonstrates how moderate levels of stress or arousal correlate with optimal learning and performance. Figure 1.1 is an adapted version of the inverted-U learning curve and helps us to understand how classroom learning can be enhanced by creating a safe emotional school climate that maintains healthy levels of stress and anxiety for students.

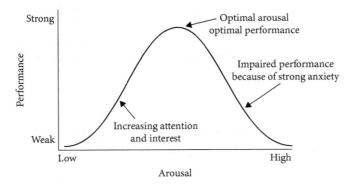

FIGURE 1.1. Inverted-U Learning Curve

The continuum of behaviors from the curve correspond with the three types of states and examples presented below (The National Institute for the Clinical Application of Behavioral Medicine, 2019; Sporleder & Forbes, 2016, p. 118):

Hyperarousal – Inability to focus or sit still, resistant to rules or directions, argumentative, impulsiveness, anxiety, overwhelmed, angry, desire to fight or flee

Regulated – Attentive, feel safe, open to learn new information, receptive, resilient, can deal with what is happening in your life, stressors are manageable and do not hinder your functioning

Hypoarousal – Defiant, shuts down, tardy or absent, avoids tasks, forgetful, disengaged, indifferent, zoned out, freeze mode, spacey, numb, withdraws from social opportunities

Siegel (2010) describes how each individual develops a unique *window of tolerance* that can help explain "how comfortable we feel with specific memories, issues, emotions, and bodily sensations. Within our window of tolerance we remain receptive; outside of it we become reactive" (p. 137). A regulated state, as described above, falls within an individual's window of tolerance, and hyperarousal or hypoarousal states signify periods of functioning outside the window of tolerance.

Based on the population and culture of any given school, various factors can contribute to an elevated level of anxiety or traumatic stress among students and school staff, including (but not limited to) violence, drugs, bullying, natural disasters, high-stakes testing, homelessness, immigration policies, physical or emotional abuse and neglect, social media, relationship or family distress, feelings of loneliness, isolation, and/or marginalization, poverty and impacts of a fluctuating economy or recession, and the state of the current sociopolitical climate.

Practice #1

Take a moment to think about what issues or experiences help you stay within your own window of tolerance and what might push you outside your window. Do you react with hyperarousal or hypoarousal behaviors or both? In the window below, label some personal experiences unique to you in which you might correspond to the designated area. Examples are provided in each section.

HYPERAROUSAL:

Inconsiderate drivers/road rage	*Fight mode, anger*	*Experiencing poor customer service*
Fear of heights; bridges	*Harm to animals*	*Unfairness/unprovoked hostility*

WINDOW OF TOLERANCE: *Regulated* *Skipping meals*	*Roller coasters* *Trying a new food*

HYPOAROUSAL:

Constant negative feedback   *Sensing favoritism/unfairness*

Reprimanded by an authority figure in front of peers

Trauma-Informed Approach

SAMHSA (2014) also offers the following description of a trauma-informed approach:

> A program, organization, or system that is trauma-informed **realizes** the widespread impact of trauma and understands potential paths for recovery; **recognizes** the signs and symptoms of trauma in clients, families, staff, and others involved with the system; and **responds** by fully integrating knowledge about trauma into policies, procedures, and practices, and seeks to actively **resist re-traumatization**. (pp. 9–10)

The four *R*s support the key assumptions of a trauma-informed approach described by SAMHSA (2014) and include:

1. Realization that all members of the community (organization, school, etc.) understand the effects of trauma and how it is integral to other systems and should be systematically addressed
2. Recognizing the signs of trauma is essential
3. Responding appropriately in applying trauma-informed principles through staff training, financial resources, and leadership
4. Resist retraumatization of students and staff (pp. 9–10)

Susan Craig (2017) additionally describes trauma-sensitive schools as "safe zones, which buffer students from external forces that threaten their potential while at the same time fostering the skills teens need to regulate internal emotions and drives" (p. 5). The drive for schools to begin shifting toward positive climates that support trauma-exposed students with learning, focus, and behavior management stems from acknowledgement that "schools are the central community for most children" (Cole et al., 2005, p. 7). Trauma-informed practices can benefit all students and school personnel, including those who are not struggling with trauma histories. This approach promotes a universal philosophy that can be effective in fostering harmonious school communities over time as a result of increased positive relationships, engagement in learning and school culture, and a sense of decreased stress levels among students, families, and staff.

Behavior Is Communication

Becoming trauma-informed means not only understanding trauma but also understanding that caring relationships are essential in fostering the positive development of youth. Children suffering from trauma do not exhibit a clear-cut list of academic and behavioral challenges, as each child's experience and response to trauma is unique. What they do have in common is the fact that living with the trauma can impede skills related to social-emotional development and lead to behavioral coping methods that may cause frustration and stress for educators. In the context of relationships, Van der Kolk (2014) explains:

> Trauma, whether it is the result of something done to you or something you yourself have done, almost always makes it difficult to engage in intimate relationships. After you have experienced something so unspeakable, how do you learn to trust yourself or anyone else again? Or, conversely, how can you surrender to an intimate relationship after you have been brutally violated? (p. 13)

In school environments, student behavior characterized as acting out is often used as a coping strategy to communicate the desire for a positive connection with an adult, and this basic relational need must be met first in order to successfully access cognition for learning (Smith & Lambert, 2008). School faculty and staff are often kept in the dark about the negative experiences some students endure outside regular school hours, and this makes it difficult for adults to understand the root of academic and behavioral challenges (Cole et al., 2005).

The idea of *caring* or *nurturing* is often misunderstood as *without consequences*, which is partly the reason why adults find it challenging to shift their perspective and approaches. The concepts of *caring/nurturing* and holding individuals *accountable* are not mutually exclusive; they are both achievable and can be quite successful through means of modeling trust and respect in a nonthreatening climate where a student's dignity remains intact. Making unmindful misinterpretations about the motivations behind a student's behavior can often unintentionally lead into dangerous territory, especially when the outcomes may be harmful to that student's future. It is essential for us to broaden our personal views of how the experiences

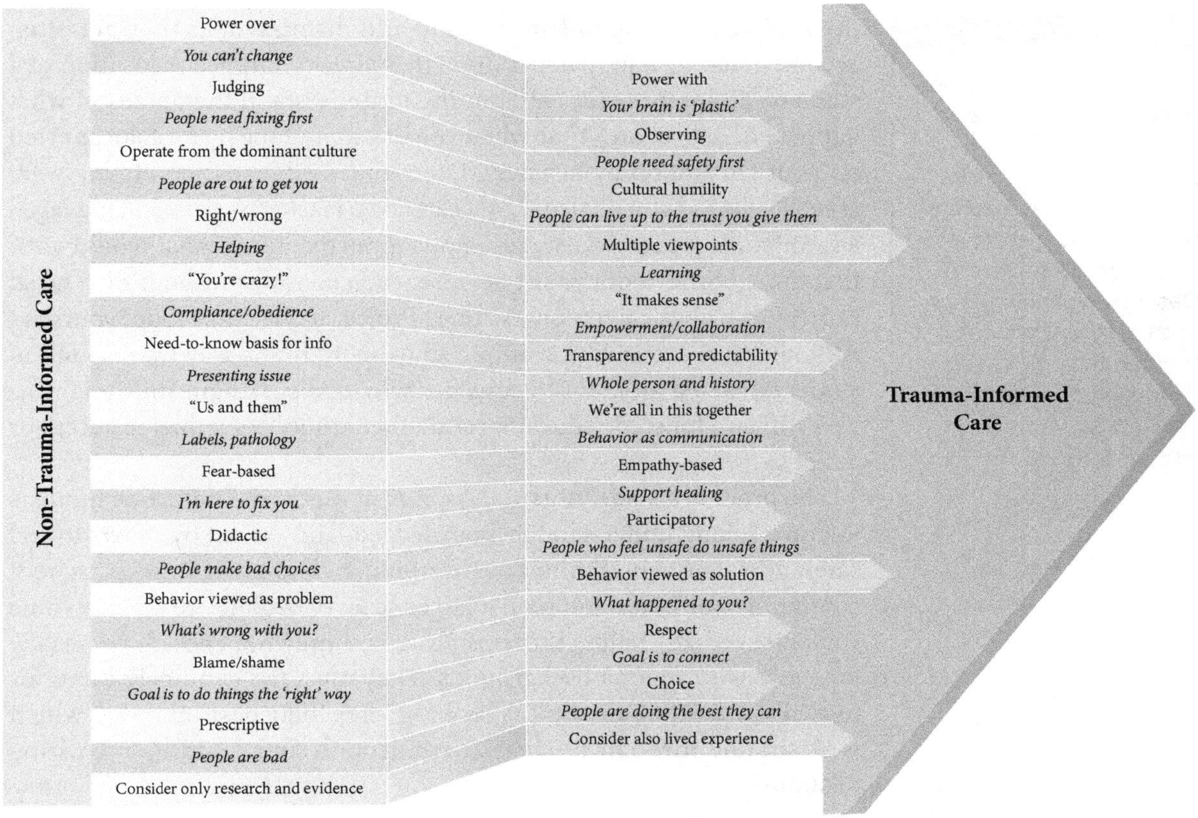

FIGURE 1.2. Trauma-Informed Care

we offer to students can trigger trauma for them, and we must look beyond our own biases to make sure we are not causing continued harm to a child who is depending on us for safety. Take a moment to read through Figure 1.2 from Echo (2017a), which provides examples of the differences between a trauma-informed and non-trauma-informed approach to responding to student behavior.

Figure 1.2 includes several interpretations of concepts that are significant to the discussions in the following chapters. From the second column of the figure, two particular mindsets that can be readily shifted and applied in our efforts toward a trauma-informed approach to students include:

1. Behavior is communication
2. What happened to you?

A common way of showing students respect and care is intentionally shifting language in a way that offers less threatening tones. An example is asking a student "What happened?" with genuine curiosity instead of the customary method of asking, in a threatening tone, "Why did you do that?" or "What's wrong with you?" These last two questions tend to leave

Reflection

What are some questions or comments you have received directly in the past that left you feeling judged or threatened and to which you may have responded defensively? Describe what elements of that experience contributed to your reaction (language, tone, nonverbals, etc.).

the recipient feeling misunderstood and dismissed, as they are often accompanied by a judgmental tone that already implies accusation of a student's ill intent before attempting to understand the details of what happened. Reflect on a time when you did something by mistake or acted on your frustration by behaving in an undesirable manner. If you were asked "Why did you do that?" by a caretaker, teacher, supervisor, manager, administrator, partner, etc. in a nonsupportive tone, what would your first thoughts be about your response when considering your own facial expressions, physical responses, tone of voice, and feelings about yourself? Although this seems like a simple adjustment in the way we respond to students, take a moment to consider why this paradigm shift might be very difficult for some educators and other school personnel to accept or adapt to.

The brain is a social organ; thus, it is in our social nature as humans to crave feeling understood, acknowledged, and valued by others to feel safe and secure enough to contribute to a class environment, school community, or other group on a larger scale (Cozolino, 2013). For some students, verbally telling them you care is simply not enough, especially for those with trauma backgrounds. They must *feel* genuinely cared for to really trust that an adult is looking after their best interests, which is attainable through nonverbal connection and building a trusting relationship.

One of the most challenging questions asked of teachers and parents is "What can you do to show or help students feel that you care about them without telling them 'I care about you' or not using words at all?" At times, the tones or actions associated with "I care about you" when resolving issues or conflicts with students can lead to students remaining unconvinced of feeling cared for based on perceptions of nonverbal ingenuity or dismissive body language and tones. The sensitivity and energy required of this task should commonly be reflected on and developed with continued practice of self-awareness from the adult.

Some general strategies that help students feel a sense of connection with school staff include taking a moment to pause and find out who students are beyond the tests and schoolwork, staying present and engaged while listening so that their insights are taken seriously, and showing respect by *helping* them understand consequences of their actions (Nelsen, 2000). Attending to the relationship through our intentional presence is a strong and effective way to reinforce to students that they matter and are worthy of our attention, regardless of academic achievement or behavioral challenges. The "Two-by-Ten" strategy has been widely used by school staff as an approach to build relationships with students who may present with difficult behavioral challenges in the classroom and entails having one-on-one conversations with students regarding whatever they desire to talk about for 2 minutes a day, 10 days in a row (Smith & Lambert, 2008). Additional strategies will be discussed later in Chapter 7.

Practice #2

Without looking back at Figure 1.2, create a chart with two columns and headings like the one below and classify each of the given terms in its respective column below: either non-trauma-informed or trauma-informed. When you are finished, continue by writing down your own adjectives, descriptions, or phrases based on your understanding of the differences between the two approaches. Share your responses with a partner or in a group to help generate more ideas for each column and practice mindsets that foster an open mind about ways to view students and each other as human beings worthy of care and respect.

curious	assumptions	hurtful	healing
harmful	"Get over it"	talk with	dismissive
demand	"What happened?"	judgments	talk at
frustrated	request	safety first	labels
expert	connect	support	"you need fixing"
empathy	right/wrong	trust	respect
bad choices	struggling	dignity	"Get tough"
caring	condescending	defiant	nurturing
"Are you okay?"	"I can't deal with you"	"Something's not right"	"I wonder what's going on"

Non-Trauma-Informed	Trauma-Informed

CASE EXAMPLE

Luis, a sixth grader, is sitting in class while his teacher is giving a science lesson. The teacher finishes teaching the 30-minute lesson, assigns related classwork for the remainder of the class period, and then takes a seat at the teacher's desk to engage in various tasks. Luis attempts to engage in the classwork but feels confused about some of the work. He does not complete the expected amount of the assignment within the allotted class time, and the teacher notices as the teacher walks around the classroom during the last few minutes of the class period. The teacher asks Luis, "Why haven't you gotten more work done?" and Luis replies, "I don't know how to do this," as he points to a particular page of his book. The teacher then replies in frustration in front of the entire class, "I just explained it, so you weren't listening. You need to pay attention."

DISCUSSION QUESTIONS

1. How do you think Luis might interpret the teacher's last statements?
2. What would your own personal thoughts or reactions be if you were Luis in this scenario?
3. What are some possible reasons why Luis did not ask for help when he did not understand some of the assignment?
4. What do you think the teacher could have done differently to help Luis feel respected and valued?

The next chapter will introduce the science behind basic neurobiology to understand how responses and interactions with students can impact behavior and have the potential to create either positive or negative relational experiences, which include possible retraumatization of earlier experiences. Having an increased knowledge base allows us to stay informed and aware of the neurological and biological processes that contribute to an individual's development and resiliency level, based on the experiences we offer through our relationships with students.

Chapter Summary

A trauma-informed learning environment offers a safe and predictable community for all students through positive support and caring adult relationships. Increased achievement disparities, school suspensions, drop-out rates, and disproportionality contribute to rising referrals of youth to the criminal justice system, signaling the urgency for systemic changes to adequately meet the needs of students (Romero, Robertson, & Warner, 2018). Emerging research on trauma continues to provide a deeper understanding of the trauma-related challenges many students face as they struggle to function successfully to meet academic, social, and emotional expectations of the educational system. Moving from punitive disciplinary measures in schools toward authentic human connection, trust, compassion, and respect is at the core of a paradigm shift fostering a positive relational culture. Developing safe and meaningful relationships with students starts with understanding that behavioral and academic challenges may stem from exposure to trauma.

Connect and Reflect

1. Looking back at Figure 1.2, reflect on your own past experiences as either a student or in a supervising role for children. What kinds of interactions translated into the left column of non-trauma-informed responses, whether you were on the giving or receiving end? What can you remember about how it may have been interpreted (facial expressions, behavior, statements, responses from surrounding peers, feelings about self, etc.)?
2. Now try and do the same reflection for the trauma-informed column. What are some notable differences in how these different styles may be received?

Extended Learning

Abel, S. A., Eggleston, K. B., Green, E. J., & Poe, S. L. (2018). *Becoming a trauma-responsive school: A guide for Virginia leaders.* Richmond, VA: Stop Child Abuse Now.

Cuellar, A. E., & Markowitz, S. (2015). School suspension and the school to prison pipeline. *International Review of Law and Economics, 43,* 98–106.

Mallett, C. A. (2016). The school-to-prison pipeline: Disproportionate impact on vulnerable children and adolescents. Retrieved from https://doi.org/10.1177/0013124516644053

Raible, J., & Irizarry, J. (2010). Redirecting the teacher's gaze: Teacher education, youth surveillance and the school-to-prison pipeline. *Teaching and Teacher Education, 26*(5), 1196–1203.

Sporleder, J., & Forbes, H. T. (2016). *The trauma-informed school: A step-by-step implementation guide for administrators and school personnel.* Boulder, CO: Beyond Consequences Institute.

Credits

Fig. 1.1: Source: https://commons.wikimedia.org/wiki/File:HebbianYerkesDodson.svg.

Fig. 1.2: Source: https://www.echoparenting.org/dev/wp-content/uploads/2018/08/Echo_Arrow_Print_8x11.pdf.

Chapter 2

The Developing Brain

I T IS OFTEN the case that adults in schools expect all students to possess the skills necessary to focus and learn the curriculum, sometimes without necessary and sufficient mental and emotional support. Since our brains are wired for interactions, every part of our brain grows in the context of relationships and people around us so that we can create mental structures and develop neural pathways based on experiences (van der Kolk, 2015). Some students experiencing high levels of stress from what is happening in their lives outside of school struggle with the unreasonable expectations to concentrate and behave *normally* (Wolpow, Johnson, Hertel, & Kincaid, 2016). The neural processes that take place during a child's early years could become severely disrupted by experiences of trauma and potentially lead to serious consequences for the child's developmental systems. Traumatic stress can cause students to respond in unhealthy ways that are harmful to physical, emotional, and mental well-being. Since most of the brain's structural and functional organization happens in childhood, experiences during this significant period heavily influence the developing brain (Perry, 2000). To better understand trauma's negative impacts on an individual's neurobiology, it is necessary to learn about some basic brain functions, the stress response system, and how they are biologically linked when students experience toxic doses of stress.

Basic Brain Functions

Since traumatic stress can cause lasting damage to the architecture and functioning of a child's developing brain, education on basic brain science is necessary for understanding the underlying neural and

Learning Objectives

1. What functions do the amygdala, prefrontal cortex, and hippocampus serve?
2. Why does the body react in fight, flight, or freeze responses?
3. How can traumatic experiences impact the stress response system?
4. How can mirror neurons positively or negatively affect a student's learning process in the school environment?

biological processes that lead to student behaviors indicative of trauma. With the existence of trauma being increasingly recognized in schools, there are several different ways to learn about the brain. One of the most common ways basic brain functions are explained is by dividing the brain into the *upstairs* and *downstairs* areas (Siegel, 2011).

Siegel and Bryson (2011) describe how the primitive *downstairs* brain is comprised of the brain stem and limbic region and is responsible for reactions, impulses, anger, strong emotions, and basic functions such as breathing. Also known as the reptilian brain, this part is developed at birth and is where an individual's basic needs are met. The more evolved *upstairs* brain contains the prefrontal cortex and is where more complex higher-order thinking occurs, such as analyzing, self-understanding, empathy, and morality (Siegel & Bryson, 2011). This area allows a child to think before acting and flourish through proper regulation of emotions during typical daily challenges and does not reach maturity until an individual reaches approximately their mid-20s. Since children's *upstairs* brains are still developing during the school years, they often get stuck in their *downstairs* brains and are not able to access the higher-level thinking required for exhibiting behaviors adults often expect of them.

Prefrontal Cortex

The prefrontal cortex (PFC) is located behind the forehead in the *upstairs brain* and is responsible for **executive functioning**, which encompasses higher-order skills that depend on a child's ability to take pause on impulses and reflect so smarter decisions can be made about how to respond. Executive functioning skills include organizing, critical thinking, working memory, planning, judgment, reasoning, problem solving, decision-making, impulse control, and focusing attention. Our PFC guides our executive functioning and also enables us to analyze, compute, predict, comprehend, evaluate, and interpret information. **Self-regulation** refers to your ability to bring your overstimulated body responses back to a state of calm and balance so you can access your PFC to reach optimal physical, emotional, and mental functioning. **Dysregulation** occurs during distressing experiences when access to the PFC becomes blocked, and your skills in accurately evaluating situations and responding mindfully are impaired. Extreme stress and overstimulation can inhibit access to the PFC, resulting in poor decisions and problematic behavior. Burke Harris (2018) explains:

> Telling a kid to sit still, concentrate, and ignore stimuli that are flooding his brain with the need to act is a lot to ask. The PFC's down-regulation can have different consequences for different people. For some, it results in an inability to concentrate and solve problems, but in others it manifests as impulsive behavior and aggression. (pp. 68–69)

Amygdala

The amygdala is an almond-shaped part of the *downstairs brain* and filters information to detect whether or not a threat exists by assessing a situation before reacting. In Figure 2.1, the amygdala receives incoming information from the body through the brain stem. If the amygdala detects a situation as safe or enjoyable, it will maintain a calm state and pass on incoming information to the PFC so it can be evaluated before a response is made. This relaxed state provides a time buffer between receiving information and responding with a good decision, allowing the PFC to examine, interpret, and arrange information. For example, when you meet someone for the first time on a blind date or you meet a new teacher on the first day of class, your amygdala helps you assess whether these people are safe or dangerous. When the amygdala scans the environment and determines there is an anticipated threat, it receives a massive amount of energy and blocks the incoming information from reaching the PFC. It also begins the process of releasing hormones that create fear and anxiety in preparation for the body to respond to the perceived stressful situation. These hormones can stay in the body for multiple days, which can become toxic.

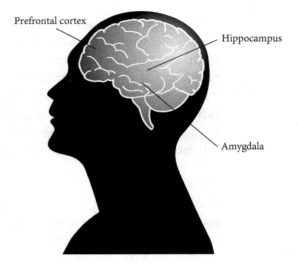

FIGURE 2.1. Basic Brain Functions

As a part of the limbic system, the amygdala is essential for regulating emotional responses and behavior such as fear, anxiety, and panic. Fear and other emotional states caused by stress prevent new information from reaching the PFC, blocking the brain's capacity for higher-level thinking and reasoning. As a result, the amygdala is left on its own to process new information and clues from the immediate environment and react accordingly with automatic *fight, flight, freeze* responses. These responses are commonly known as "flipping your lid" (Siegel & Bryson, 2011, pp. 43, 62–63) and happen when the amygdala is activated, blocking the connection between the *upstairs* and *downstairs* areas. When you notice a student is in their *downstairs* brain because they are angry, scared, panicked, reactive, etc., the main goal should be to get the student back to a sense of safety by calming their amygdala. This can successfully be achieved through moments of authentic trust in the relationship where the student feels seen and heard. Chapter 3 will discuss attachment relationships as they relate to a sense of security and safety with a parent or other adult.

Link Box

Access Daniel Siegel's short video titled *Flipping Your Lid* through the link below. This is a common method used to teach brain science to school staff and students:

https://www.youtube.com/watch?v=GoT_2NNoC68&t=1s

The amygdala does not distinguish between actual and perceived threats, which means it can create a false sense of danger that alerts the body to react with potentially challenging behaviors. When the body reacts before the PFC can think reasonably about information or the current situation, this can be problematic when such behavior seems unwarranted in the context of what is happening. The fear that develops from an overstimulated amygdala can cause behaviors such as hypervigilance, meltdowns, exaggerated reactions to mistakes, and hyperarousal. When the amygdala and other brain areas become damaged by early childhood trauma and neglect, individuals have difficulty distinguishing between who is safe and who is dangerous (van der Kolk, 2015).

Hippocampus

The hippocampus is part of a seahorse-shaped pair located close to the center of the brain and is associated with arousal. It is also essential for storing memory and learning as well as the recovery and translation of such information, such as spatial recall. These functions can help us with controlling our responses to fear and threats through the processing of emotional information; however, high levels of stress may impair memory and retention of learning. A child with excess neural activation from a perceived threat has the potential for altered brain development, which may result in changes in emotional, behavioral, and cognitive functioning (Perry, 2001). Because the hippocampus is vulnerable to stress, elevated levels of stress hormones from trauma can cause it to decrease in volume. When a child feels consistently threatened, chronic activation of the stress response system can lead to deterioration of the hippocampus (Perry, 2000).

Fight, Flight, Freeze

When possible danger is detected, the body reacts in a defensive mode to ensure chances of survival. An increase in heart rate and blood flow toward muscles helps prepare the body for the possibility of fighting or running away from a serious threat. This hyperarousal state is meant to be a temporary and beneficial way for the body to adapt to situations. Trauma can cause a child to continuously be on high alert, activating into fight, flight, or freeze mode and losing capability for logical thinking. Children with trauma histories may not be capable of regulating their emotional states or depending on others for help and may not be able to integrate incoming information, resulting in disorganized behaviors (Streeck-Fischer & van der Kolk, 2000). Romero, Robertson, and Warner (2018) describe the impacts of trauma on children's behavior and neural development related to fight, flight, and freeze responses:

> They will often have an exaggerated and impulsive response of fight, flight, or freeze. Fight responses in the classroom can look like the externalizing behaviors that we mentioned, such as defiance, impulsivity, and aggression. Freeze and flight responses can appear more like internalized behaviors such as shutting down, withdrawal, anxiety, or depression. Meanwhile, they will not have access to the parts of their brain, such as the prefrontal cortex, that would help them to reason, think flexibly, and respond more appropriately. (p. 69)

What physical changes do you notice about your own body when your amygdala is activated from reacting to a threat or danger? What about a pleasurable situation?

Other Functions Affected by Trauma

As you continue your own learning about stress and trauma in the school setting, professional development opportunities will enable you to delve into deeper concepts beyond this introductory text and enhance your existing knowledge about these topics. Your increased level of experience and expertise will eventually impact your confidence in your approaches and reduce any fears about how to handle tough situations and model appropriate practices for your colleagues and students. Your patience, understanding, and willingness to be okay with the unknown during potentially stressful situations will become one of your most valuable tools in your career as an educator and role model. Brief descriptions of additional functions are provided below. You will most likely encounter them throughout current and future literature or professional development related to childhood trauma:

> **Corpus Callosum**—This band of nerves fully develops by age 12 and connects the left and right hemispheres of the brain, allowing for communication between sides so complex information can be processed and physical coordination can be maintained. Individuals with histories of abuse and neglect have been found with decreased capacities of the corpus callosum (Abel, Eggleston, Green, & Poe, 2018). This decrease in size impairs brain activity and learning and is associated with sleep issues in children (Wolpow, Johnson, Hertel, & Kincaid, 2016).

> **Occipital Lobe**—This part of the brain is associated with processing of vision. Witnessing domestic violence can cause reduction of density and thickness, with the most critical impacts between ages 11 and 13 (Teicher, Samson, Anderson, & Ohashi, 2016).

> **Hypothalamus**—This is located in the center of the brain and is activated by experiences of extreme stress and trauma. It prompts the adrenal glands to generate stress hormones and physically impacts the brain.

Hypothalamic-Pituitary-Adrenal (HPA) Axis—Initiates cortisol production by the adrenal glands. Cortisol is a stress hormone that helps the body adapt to long-term stressors (Burke Harris, 2018).

Sympatho-Adrenomedullary (SAM) Axis—Initiates adrenaline and noradrenaline production by the adrenal glands. Adrenaline and noradrenaline are stress hormones that help prime the body to be ready for immediate responses to stressful situations (Burke Harris, 2018).

The Stress Response System

Stress is described as physical, mental, or emotional strain or tension (Wolpow, Johnson, Hertel, & Kincaid, 2016). We learned from the inverted-U learning curve in Chapter 1 that a manageable level of stress can motivate us to be productive and focus on completing tasks, while an excessive amount of stress can lead to inefficiency, high anxiety, and poor health. One of the ways the brain survives is it "learns and remembers our experiences of reward, punishment, success, and failure to apply to future situations" (Cozolino, 2013, p. 73). The stress response system is a way for our bodies to protect us, as it focuses on identifying all the stimuli connected with dangerous experiences or situations so it can access previous experiences to know how to respond. Future encounters associated with these sensory reminders can cause the body to generate warning signs, such as increased heart rate and muscle tension.

When we experience either perceived or genuine threats, the hormone **cortisol** is released in the body. A minimal level of cortisol in the brain helps us maintain positive health and a state of alertness. Chronic and excessive amounts of cortisol from experiencing physical, emotional, or environmental stress for prolonged periods can have detrimental effects on a child's brain, negatively impacting cognition, memory, and the ability to absorb new information, which means that stressed brains are resistant to learning (Cozolino, 2013). Difficulty with thinking and remembering information during a highly stressful situation is an example of high cortisol levels hindering proper functioning of the brain, which can also cause harm to the hippocampus.

The National Scientific Council on the Developing Child (2004) describes stress by classifying three different biological responses and each of their effects on a child's developing systems. It is important to understand the value of practicing experiences of positive and tolerable stress, as described in Figure 2.2.

We need to recognize that not all stress is bad, that children require challenges and risk as well as safety. ... Children's brains are shaped by what they do slowly and repeatedly over time. If they don't have the chance to practice coping with small risks and dealing with the consequences of those choices, they won't be well prepared for making larger and far more consequential decisions. ... We need to allow children to try and fail. ... At the same time, we also need to provide balance by not setting policies that will magnify one mistake. (Perry, 2006, pp. 239–240)

POSITIVE	TOLERABLE	TOXIC
Stress Response	Stress Response	Stress Response
• Normal, essential part of healthy development • Increased heart rate and adrenaline • Heightens focus	• Activates body's alert system • Longer lasting than positive stress response but time limited • Buffered by at least one caring and responsive adult that provides a sense of security and protection • Temporary effects if secure support system is in place • Child's brain and organ systems can recover from potentially harmful impacts	• Strong, frequent, prolonged activation of stress • Disrupts development of brain architecture and other organ systems • Increased risk for impaired learning and behavior • Adequate stress buffer (adult) is not available
Examples: Receiving injected immunizations, first time left with a new caregiver	Examples: Loss of loved one, natural disaster	Examples: Recurring physical or emotional abuse, chronic neglect, severe poverty, caregiver substance abuse or mental illness, exposure to violence

FIGURE 2.2. Three Types of Stress Responses (National Scientific Council on the Developing Child, 2004)

In contrast, toxic stress responses can be activated when a child does not receive sufficient caring support from adults, which is necessary for adapting to healthy functioning of regulation systems. Excessive and prolonged experiences of stress that affect brain growth and other organ systems can have serious long-term consequences on learning, behavior, and health (National Scientific Council on the Developing Child, 2004). Streeck-Fischer and van der Kolk (2000) explain that "If children are exposed to unmanageable stress and if the caregiver does not take over the function of modulating the child's arousal ... exposure to family violence, the child will be unable to organize and categorize its experiences in a coherent fashion" (p. 907).

The reality of our current societal and political climates presents a capacity for numerous stressors that more and more young children are exposed to. The potential danger associated with future health outcomes for these youth comes with well-intentioned systems in place that lack awareness and understanding of its harmful consequences. Some of these stressors include:

- Minimal unstructured playtime or downtime
- Consistently chaotic or overstimulating environments
- Pressure to overachieve
- Anxiety associated with comparing self to others
- Unrealistic parent expectations
- Family conflicts or dysfunction

Reflection

Based on your experience(s) working with children or your own memories of childhood, what other stressors can you add to this list that may cause high levels of cortisol to be released in the body?

Wolpow, Johnson, Hertel, and Kincaid (2016, p. 10) describe how a child's developing neural processes can be altered through the body's responses to stress and fear if that child consistently experiences an environment composed of threat, chaos, instability, and trauma:

> Put more simply, the brain develops and organizes in reaction to how it is stimulated. The experience of the child affected by trauma is fear, threat, unpredictability, frustration, chaos, hunger, and pain. Traumatic stress overstimulates the brain. This pattern of overstimulation alters the child's neurobiology to adapt to the high-stress pattern.

Childhood trauma literally changes an individual's neural wiring. It is confusing for a child to feel terrified by a caretaker who is hurting them when the child is supposed to depend on that adult for protection and safety. When a child's developing brain is trying to create an identity and make sense of experiencing such a hurtful and perplexing relationship, the child can develop serious issues with health and functioning, such as depression, irritability, insomnia, and difficulty maintaining relationships (Esrick, 2018).

Neuroplasticity

The capacity of the brain to change is called **neuroplasticity** and occurs when new or familiar experiences create neural firing patterns in the brain, linking previously disconnected areas toward strengthening and adaptation (Siegel, 2010). Burke Harris (2018) explains how the brain rewires or reorganizes itself and changes in response to patterned, repetitive experiences: "The growing and changing of neurons and synapses can happen in response to injury, exercise, hormones, emotion, learning, and even thinking. Our brains are always changing in response to our experiences" (p. 145). This is an example of the notion that *what fires together, wires together* (Hebb, 1949), which refers to the neural connections that fire together to strengthen neural pathways based on repeated positive or negative experiences. The more frequently a positive or negative experience is repeated, the stronger the neural networks become in creating patterns of expectations and mental states. For example, consistently practicing a sport creates positive changes in the brain, promoting strong neural networks that help you improve your skills. Negative wiring in the brain can be strengthened by receiving daily doses of pessimistic responses from a teacher. Perry (2006) explains: "These facts are wonderful when what we are considering repeating is loving and nurturing, but they are frankly terrifying when we think about violence and the increasing number of simulations of violence that surround us and our children" (p. 240). Adults in schools can either strengthen or disrupt the neural wiring of our students based on how they experience us and how we make them feel through our interactions.

Link Box

Access a short video by Daniel Siegel titled *Connecting to Calm* using the link below. This provides an example of how adults can calm a child's amygdala through caring connection:

https://www.youtube.com/watch?v=aV3hp_eaoiE

Practice #1

Successful communication with parents and caretakers can be developed through experience and attained by demonstrating patience and willingness to listen to their needs, concerns, and frustrations. In the video you just viewed, Siegel mentioned how the sequencing of approaches is very important for helping to calm an individual's amygdala. Parents and caretakers may approach you for various reasons during times of distress, signaling their need for your help when their lids might be "flipped." Before you are tempted to problem solve with your analytical brain, try to practice the technique of human connection and care before starting to problem solve. It may take some extra minutes to stop, slow down, and allow the other person to feel heard and understood, but the benefits can include experiences of authentic, positive connection and improved skills in building relationships with families.

Using the following email template as a guide, draft a response to a parent you have never met in person who has sent you an email with an extremely unpleasant tone. Face-to-face communication is often a better way to resolve an issue with an individual who is angry, as use of email limits opportunities for genuine connection and energy that is felt from being in each other's presence. Both parties may also be able to use nonverbal communication in the process of calming, feeling understood, and building or restoring a relationship. In this exercise, the parent is upset and expecting a prompt response because their child has been coming home lately and reporting they are constantly being bullied by a peer and nothing has been done to address the bullying. This is the first time you are hearing about this situation, and you have been completely unaware of any bullying behavior between these students. The template serves as a guide, as variations would be suitable to address different issues, including positive situations. Feel free to add or modify parts that reflect your own personality and writing style while maintaining professionalism and the sequencing of validation and connection before problem solving.

Mirror Neurons

Kirke Olson (2014) describes how students have the remarkable capability to "borrow" a teacher's prefrontal cortex or state of mind by the type of climate the teacher offers. This process of intentionally lending students our state of calm through our presence and attunement in turn calms students' nervous systems so they are able to demonstrate openness and flexibility. It can also be just as effective as unintentionally lending them our state of

Dear (Parent),

Thank you for contacting me: *regarding ...*

                                                               About ...

I'm sorry to hear that (you/student/family) is: *having difficulty with ...*

                                                               struggling with ...

                                                               not feeling supported in ...

                                                               feeling _____ about ...

(This must have been/This must be) (frustrating/stressful/etc.) for (you/student/family) to experience _____.

(I/we) will check in with _____ to: *see what happened*

                                                               make sure _____ is feeling okay

                                                               make sure everything is okay

I appreciate you contacting me about this and also your trust in communicating any concerns.

Sincerely,

_____

negativity, dismissiveness, impatience, judgment, etc. Modeling the qualities of attunement and trauma-informed approaches through our way of being (calm, patience, undivided attention, an open mind, curiosity, unconditional care, etc.) in a genuine and patient manner helps transform the surrounding energy into one of safety, trust, and connectedness. Perry (2009) describes how an intentional and compassionate way of being can help with healing from impacts of toxic stress and trauma:

> Then, and today, the presence of familiar people projecting the social-emotional cues of acceptance, compassion, caring, and safety calms the stress response of the individual: "You are one of us, you are welcome, you are safe." This powerful positive effect of healthy relational interactions on the individual—mediated by the relational and stress-response neural systems—is at the core of relationally based protective mechanisms that help us survive and thrive following trauma and loss. Individuals who have few positive relational interactions during or after trauma have a much more difficult time decreasing the trauma-induced activation of the stress response systems and therefore will be much more likely to have ongoing symptoms. (p. 246)

Mirror neurons are cells that fire together to form neural networks when we observe others and learn from watching their actions, and Cozolino (2013) describes it in this way: "our brains actually practice doing what we are watching others do and we become motivated to imitate in order to attain the same reward" (p. 141). Additionally, Siegel (2013) describes mirror neurons as *soaking up* the feelings and emotions of others through our experiences of them. When a student watches another individual behave in a certain way, their brain cells have the capacity to "fire" together when they experience engaging in the same action; this is also known in the interpersonal neurobiology field as *what fires together, wires together* (Hebb, 1949). This is especially important for school staff members to understand because our modeling of behaviors and attitudes strongly guides the behavior of our students and places much emphasis on relationships in relation to learning. For example, students may strongly dislike a certain subject yet enjoy that particular class because they soak up the contagious positive energy the teacher provides during lessons and in the classroom in general. Students have the ability to mirror the feelings, intentions, emotions, attitudes, gestures, actions, etc. of others through watching and observing their behavior. This resonating with others' emotions can have either positive or negative outcomes, including when it is activated between students. Perry (2006b) suggests that "Another important implication of our mirrored biology is that concentrating children with aggressive or impulsive tendencies together is a bad idea, as they will tend to reflect and magnify this, rather than calming each other" (p. 245).

Understanding mirror neurons allows us to recognize how our own stress responses can either consciously or unconsciously impact the anxiety of our students. In other words, school staff and faculty members potentially have the power and capability to dictate whether student brains will be ready to take in new information and increase academic performance. This includes every single adult a student encounters throughout the school day, such as bus drivers, maintenance staff, cafeteria employees, instructional assistants/paraprofessionals, office staff, etc. Mirror neurons can also impact connections from student to student, as student attitudes and states of reactivity can potentially influence a group's momentum toward negative or positive climates and relationships.

CASE EXAMPLE

Liam is a third-grade student in a public elementary school, and his older sister, Esther, attends the local middle school. Liam and Esther are first-generation children in the United States, and their biological parents are of Asian descent. They both received ELL services in their first 2 years of attending the public schools. Their family owns a local grocery store and has lived in the community ever since Esther was an infant. The parents have always been known to volunteer at the school when overall parent participation has been minimal. Esther has maintained her reputation as an excellent student academically and behaviorally throughout elementary school and into middle school. Liam has also performed well academically since kindergarten; however, his current teacher, Ms. Holbrook, notices that Liam is beginning to struggle a little with academics, especially with focusing and following instructions. Ms. Holbrook also observes Liam experiences many challenges in social interactions with his peers this year, especially during group work and unstructured recess time. One morning during recess, Liam has a disagreement with a few classmates over wanting to choose the game they play. Ms. Holbrook walks over to help resolve the situation and then impatiently pulls Liam aside to talk to him, as she is frustrated by the excessive frequency of these discussions with Liam about making good choices. Liam begins to cry as he maintains eye contact with Ms. Holbrook while she lectures him about making good choices, and he says, "I have no friends. Nobody wants to be my friend."

Reflection

Pause for a moment before you continue to read the rest of this case example. At this point, do you see Liam through a trauma-informed lens (*Something's going on here, and I wonder what's happening*) or not through a trauma-informed lens (*Liam is choosing to behave a certain way, so that is why he has no friends*)?

Later that day, Ms. Holbrook decides to consult with Ms. Jacobson, the new school counselor this year, about supporting Liam emotionally when he becomes overwhelmed and dysregulated during these interpersonal conflicts. Ms. Holbrook shares that it has been difficult trying to communicate with Liam's mother, since English is not her primary language, and that their father died in a tragic motor vehicle accident while riding his bicycle last year. Liam's mom has been extremely busy lately as a single parent while trying to maintain their family's business and has not been seen volunteering in the school since the accident. Ms. Jacobson does not know Liam well yet. She coordinates with Ms. Holbrook to set aside time to meet with Liam privately in her office the following day so she can start building rapport and getting to know Liam better.

In the meantime, Ms. Jacobson checks in with Liam's second-grade teacher, Mr. Martinez, to get a sense of what Liam's academic and social-emotional functioning was like last year. Ms. Jacobson learns from Mr. Martinez and her earlier consultation with Ms. Holbrook that there have been some noticeable differences in Liam's social, emotional, and academic functioning since his father died. Mr. Martinez also makes a point to mention a potentially subtle yet noticeable change in Liam's eyes compared to last year. When asked to elaborate about this, Mr. Martinez describes how recently, it seems one of Liam's eyes may be slightly crossed and may not be noticeable to some people because it is minimal, but Mr. Martinez notices it when they regularly greet each other and make eye contact in passing. Mr. Martinez thanks Ms. Jacobson for checking in about Liam and says, "I wasn't sure, and I know it's not my place because I'm not a medical professional, but it feels like something is a little different with Liam's eyes. And it's hard to notice, but I notice."

Ms. Jacobson meets with Liam the next day in her office. Liam is very curious about Ms. Jacobson and asks many questions about her role in the school and her personal life. After chatting and learning about each other for a while, Ms. Jacobson asks Liam about what his life is like at home. Liam shares that he has to go to their family's grocery store after school and that he does his homework in a back room. He then goes on to explain that when he gets something wrong on his homework, his mom hits him on the back of his head, right in between his ears. Liam states that it doesn't leave a bruise or bleed or anything like that, but it feels pretty hard, and it happens a lot. At the end of their meeting, Ms. Jacobson thanks Liam for spending time with her and walks him out to the hallway. Liam sincerely looks up at Ms. Jacobson, waves bye, and walks away toward his classroom. Ms. Jacobson walks into her office and closes the door. She looks up the phone number to the local Child Protective Services (CPS) office and picks up the phone.

DISCUSSION QUESTIONS

1.   What part(s) of the brain do you think are affected most by Liam being hit on the back of his head between the ears? How might this impact his learning and any other functioning in school?

2.   Do you think it is helpful for Ms. Holbrook to repeatedly have conversations with Liam about making good choices when he is dysregulated? Why or why not?

3.   Discuss your thoughts about Liam possibly having disciplinary consequences in school for behaviors as a result of cognitive and emotional impairments that developed from the physical abuse.

Chapter Summary

Learning about basic brain science is helpful for a better understanding of behaviors. As we continue to understand different processes associated with trauma, consider your own perspective on learning and behavior management. The process of acquiring a trauma-informed lens requires time for self-reflection and a willingness to have an open mind about the possibility of discomfort, as we cannot begin to try to help a child heal if we are unable to acknowledge that there may be times when we may need our own support to get back to a calm state. Having a trauma lens requires constant awareness around our own emotions, especially when they have the power to influence a student's attitude toward learning and school.

Connect and Reflect

1.   Oftentimes, in a school setting, staff members worry about how to approach parents or caregivers about an incident or ongoing challenge their child is struggling with in the school. It can be very intimidating for educators when the school is initiating contact with the caregiver to communicate information that may possibly not be received well. Sometimes you may come across an irate parent who is expecting you to follow up with them. Whether the contact is through email, by phone, or in person, the unpredictability of how caregivers will react can cause much anxiety for adults in schools. If you have already established a solid relationship with a family, it is usually much easier to communicate with them, since a level of trust has already been formed. Based on what you learned about the *upstairs* and *downstairs* brain, how would you attempt to calm the amygdala of a parent who is dysregulated when you can see their brain has shut off access to their PFC from the way the parent is reacting? First, explain what strategies you would use if you were face to face with a parent, and then describe your approach if you were calling the parent on the phone.

2.   Have you ever received an email or text that caused you to "flip your lid" and you discovered later that you understood the message incorrectly or out of context? How did you react, and what happened afterward?

3.   Describe a situation in the past when your amygdala blocked access to your PFC and you reacted unfavorably. What helped to calm your own *downstairs* brain?

Extended Learning

Cozolino, L. (2013). *The social neuroscience of education: Optimizing attachment & learning in the classroom.* New York, NY: W.W. Norton & Company.

Hoffman, K., Cooper, G., & Powell, B. (2017). *Raising a secure child: How circle of security parenting can help you nurture your child's attachment, emotional resilience, and freedom to explore.* New York, NY: Guilford Press.

Olson, K. (2014). *The invisible classroom: Relationships, neuroscience & mindfulness in schools.* New York, NY: W.W. Norton & Company.

Siegel, D. J. (2011). *The whole-brain child: 12 revolutionary strategies to nurture your child's developing mind.* New York, NY: Bantam Books.

Van der Kolk, B. A. (2014). *The body keeps the score: Brain, mind, and body in the healing of trauma.* New York, NY: Viking.

Credits

Chapter 3

Attachment Patterns

ATTACHMENT IS A TERM used to describe the complex study of relationships and human connection, and research on this relevant topic continues to evolve from various disciplines of science. Child Welfare Information Gateway, the Children's Bureau, and FRIENDS National Resource Center for Community-Based Child Abuse Prevention (2019) describe attachment as "the relationship that develops as a result of a caregiver's sensitive attention to a child and the child's responses to the caregiver" (p. 6). From birth, children are biologically driven to attach and begin developing coping styles to get their needs met by parents/caregivers. Attachments are formed based on the level of safety, comfort, and nurturance provided by such adults during childhood. The social brain yearns for connection with attachment figures and creates a sense of how our own earlier experiences of attachment with caretakers help shape our behaviors, emotions, and perceptions of how we view the world and how we see ourselves in relation to the world (Siegel, 2013). This sense of self can heavily influence how we respond and interact in our relationships with others, and this shaping of the brain has the potential to hinder or support an individual's development in learning how to navigate through life.

Having some basic knowledge about attachment models can help adults who work with children develop a deeper understanding about the impacts of establishing and maintaining positive relationships, as positive attachment relationships are a significant component of protecting individuals from some of the harmful effects of trauma (van der Kolk, 2015). These models serve as a way for our brains to organize how we approach relationships and our interactions as we continue to learn and develop as human beings. Just as you cannot

Learning Objectives

1. What are the four *Ss* of attachment?
2. What is the Strange Situation?
3. What are the different types of attachment patterns that evolved from the Strange Situation?
4. How can early attachment patterns affect future relationships?
5. What is the connection between attachment and complex trauma?
6. How does shame impact a child's development?
7. What are the differences among guilt, shame, and core shame?

fully grasp how to write a simple paragraph without understanding the elements of basic sentence structure, basic knowledge of attachment models is essential to developing awareness of how our relationships with students and the experiences we provide them can significantly influence their development. As adults in schools begin to shift their perspective to understand that behavior is communication, it will be possible to nurture the emerging need to support students exhibiting behavior that is symptomatic of trauma. Appreciating the value of learning about attachment models can empower us to approach our work with patience and confidence in our abilities to cultivate meaningful connections with students *and* colleagues or other individuals in our lives. It may also enable us to recognize the endless opportunities available to personally experience how our actions and interactions with students have the power to influence their neural wiring in positive or negative ways.

This chapter will provide a basic introduction to patterns of attachment and discuss how unresolved attachment issues have the potential to heavily influence an individual through childhood, adolescence, and later into adulthood. The lack of a secure attachment figure or a weak connection with a caregiver during early years has the capacity to create so much hurt that a child may grow to feel and believe that safety with any other individual is impossible, possibly developing into complex trauma. Children with a history of caretaker relationships characterized by chronic unresponsiveness or rejection develop an enduring fear of being left alone and vulnerable (Howes & Ritchie, 2002). In schools, our attachment patterns as adults impact how we respond to students and various situations as we take on roles similar to parents/caretakers in an educational setting. We will then consider how these models can potentially become activated or reactivated through teacher–student relationships in the classroom as well as in relationships with other school faculty and staff. The concept of shame will also be explored, as its detrimental effects on emotional safety for students ultimately impacts their ability to learn, especially those with a trauma background. This discussion will help us begin to shift our perspective toward developing a thoughtful understanding of motivation behind behavior and allow us to reflect on our own histories of attachment through our responses to students and what hidden messages they may be receiving from us.

Strange Situation

A British psychiatrist named John Bowlby contributed extensive research on human attachment through his trilogy of work titled *Attachment and Loss* (1973, 1980, 1982). In this research, Bowlby focused on the complexities of relational connections between mothers and infants, discovering that variations exist regarding patterns of attachment in such early phases of life. Bowlby found that leaving a child alone without the mother in the presence of a stranger created a level of distress in the child, where the child's behavior upon reunification with the mother revealed a sense of whether the child experienced a soothing or stressful relationship with the mother based on their interactions.

Mary Ainsworth and a team of colleagues further developed Bowlby's work through groundbreaking research on infant attachment presented in *Patterns of Attachment: A Psychological*

Study of the Strange Situation (1978). These significant contributions to the field of attachment by Bowlby and Ainsworth uncovered a wealth of observations and insights expanding on relationships related to early experiences in combination with primary caregiver interactions. Using a method known as the infant strange situation, Ainsworth's research team began each observation by placing a mother with her 1-year-old child in an unfamiliar playroom. A stranger was then sent into the room, and the mother left the child in the playroom with the stranger for a few minutes. After some time, the mother returned to the playroom, and the child's behavior toward the parent was observed. The infants displayed either secure or nonsecure attachments through their responses toward the mothers after they returned to the playroom, and from these findings, infant attachment behavior was categorized into different models.

Secure Attachment

Bowlby discovered that children instinctively form a primary attachment bond with an adult, and this attachment serves as the secure base or safe haven that enables a child to feel confident enough to explore the world and develop autonomy through trusting and mutually rewarding relationships. Developing secure attachments to caregivers is essential for children, as "a strong and secure emotional bond between children and their caregivers is critical for children's physical, social, and emotional development, including their ability to form trusting relationships and to exhibit positive behaviors" (Child Welfare Information Gateway, Children's Bureau, & FRIENDS National Resource Center for Community-Based Child Abuse Prevention, 2019, p. 6). In the strange situation, securely attached infants were able to use their mothers as secure bases for exploring the unfamiliar environment. These infants exhibited distress when their mothers left the playroom and shifted back to comfort from relief once the mothers returned, demonstrating the capacity to anticipate being easily soothed by their mothers based on earlier interactions. The infants were enthusiastic about returning to play after reconnecting with their mothers, indicating the children had enough consistent experiences of safety and security in their relationships to feel confident in taking risks and exploring with uncertainty. The mother had established herself as a safe haven, providing comfort to the child by letting the child know they will be welcomed back warmly with open arms when they feel the need to reconnect with their mother again. The infant's brain is able to grow in healthy ways through continuous experiences of disruption and repair. A self-image is then developed through the infant's expectation that any states of distress will soon be relieved, because in the child's mind, they can consistently depend on a parent/caretaker to soothe the distress and help them feel okay (van der Kolk, 2015).

Daniel Siegel offers simple and insightful ways of understanding attachment in *Parenting From the Inside Out* (2003), and his common use of acronyms helps parents, educators, and other professionals who work with children to easily grasp the relevance of our roles in influencing brain development to support behavior, emotional regulation, healthy relationship patterns, and resilience. The **ABCs of Attachment** is a way Siegel describes how secure attachment is developed between a parent/caretaker and child. *Attunement* is connecting with a child in a way that makes them feel understood, which is often strengthened and shared through caring nonverbal communication. This attunement with a caretaker leads to the child developing regulation of the body, emotions, and states of mind through an internal sense of *balance* that is supported by consistent connection. The child then experiences a sense of *coherence* through the relationship with the caretaker that allows the capacity for feeling integrated and connected within the self and with others.

A second way that Siegel (2003) summarizes secure human attachment needs is through the **Four Ss of Attachment**, which are four concepts beginning with the letter *S* that easily enable us to conceptualize what a secure relationship looks like. The first need is to be *seen*, which involves a sense that our caregiver is paying attention to our cry for comfort through our behavior and nonverbal communication and is offering a reassuring response that meets our need to feel heard, understood, and felt. When a child's chronic experience is trying to be seen and have others respond to them to no avail, the child's brain and stress hormones become extremely dysregulated and can have negative impacts on biological and psychological development (van der Kolk, 2015). The second need is feeling *safe*, which translates into feeling that our caregiver protects us from danger without also feeling terrified by them. The ability to be *soothed* is the third need, where our moments of distress can easily be calmed by how our caregiver responds to us, and we feel better because of it. If the first three Ss are met, then a child senses these experiences with their caregiver as a *secure* relationship that ultimately develops into a positive self-image and expectation of others, empathy, self-regulation, and a drive to become a contributing member of society. A secure attachment model suggests that the four Ss of attachment have consistently been met through early caregiver interactions, where the child has internalized their caregiver as a source of comfort and safety through expectations that the caregiver will be present, caring, accommodating, and supportive of the child's independence as they continue through stages of development.

Children's development depends on their experiences of the relationships with adults around them and is driven by a reciprocal process called *serve and return*, which is characterized by a mutual desire for responsive communication between a child and adult (National Scientific Council on the Developing Child, 2004). The ability for individuals to be in sync with each other, such as moving or singing together, activates synchronous pathways and provides a powerful way for the brain to organize itself (van der Kolk, 2015). Having healthy early attachment experiences allows an individual to maintain trust in relationships, self-regulate, and exercise intellectual and emotional intelligence (Cozolino, 2014). Siegel (2014) explains that

> it's never too late to create positive change in a child's life. Studies also demonstrate that a nurturing relationship with someone other than a parent in which the child feels understood and safe provides an important source of resilience, a seed in the child's mind that can be developed later on as the child grows. Relationships with relatives, teachers, childcare providers, and counselors can provide an important source of connection for the growing child. These relationships don't replace a secure attachment with a primary caregiver, but they are a source of strength for the child's developing mind. (p. 107)

Link Box

See additional resources below to help increase your understanding about secure attachment:

1. A brief 3-minute video excerpt featuring Ed Tronick and titled *Still Face Experiment: Dr. Edward Tronick* (2007), which is available on YouTube at https://www.youtube.com/watch?v=apzXGEbZhto&t=8s

2. A 6-minute video titled *How-to: 5 Steps for Brain-Building Serve and Return* (2019) from the Center on the Developing Child website at https://developingchild.harvard.edu/resources/how-to-5-steps-for-brain-building-serve-and-return/?utm_source=newsletter&utm_medium=email&utm_campaign=june_2019

After watching these videos, discuss some of the behaviors you observed from the adults that helped soothe the child to create a climate of safety and trust in the relationship.

Insecure Attachment

Avoidant

Ainsworth and her colleagues found two additional attachment patterns that fall under the category of *insecure attachment*. Insecure attachment is characterized by a child's inability to feel comforted or soothed by others and develops from distressing early experiences with a caretaker that prevent a sense of safety within relationships (Cozolino, 2014). At times, avoidantly attached infants did the opposite of those who were found to be securely attached in this situation; they did not depend on the mothers for a secure base when exploring the unfamiliar environment and exhibited minimal distress when their mothers were not present in the room. Once their mothers returned to the room, these infants avoided them and showed no interested in seeking comfort, behaving indifferently to both the mothers and strangers.

These avoidantly attached infants experienced a dismissive style of parenting with a lack of being seen or soothed in their early relationships with their mothers, resulting in consistent patterns of emotional disconnection with such parents. As a result, these infants' brains developed a learned expectation that they need to emotionally take care of themselves, since they could not emotionally get what they needed from their mothers: ultimately, a sense of feeling soothed and safe. These continued experiences that people do not come to one's rescue generate a self-image described by expectations of *I can't count on others, so I have to learn how to do it myself* (van der Kolk, 2015). This learned attachment response is a way for the child to adapt and survive the best they can with what they have been given, as the child may feel it is much easier to self-regulate than to deal with the distressing feelings the disconnection with the mother provides. One consequence of this emotional self-dependency is that these infants in the strange situation had not yet experienced adequate connections with their caregivers to learn the value of relationships. As an attempt to minimize attachment needs, this coping style has the potential to instinctively and sometimes unconsciously maintain a world view that is driven by disconnected feelings from others as well as disconnection from one's own emotional needs.

Anxious/Ambivalent

Like securely attached infants, the anxiously/ambivalently attached infants showed distress once their mothers left the room. However, a recognizable difference is that these infants became worried and anxious about their mothers' availability in the unfamiliar environment before they left the room. Upon the mothers' return to the playroom, these infants had difficulty with being soothed and took longer to return to play. They responded to their mothers by clinging or showing anger or resistance and were less inclined to explore the unfamiliar environment due to uncertainty about whether their needs were going to be met. This confusing inconsistency in what to expect from a mother developed from earlier patterns of interactions that created an internal anxiety in which a lot of the children's energy was spent worrying about whether they would be soothed or would need to take on some of their mothers' own anxiety or fear.

Disorganized/Disoriented

In later research, Mary Main and Erik Hesse (1990) observed some infant responses consisting of intense, inconsistent reactions to their mothers when they returned to the playroom. Categorized as a third insecure attachment style called the disorganized/disoriented model, these infants' unexpected behaviors did not suitably match any of the three previous attachment styles. Some observations of infant behaviors included walking toward their mothers with heads looking away, falling to the ground, freezing, or rocking.

In this attachment model, the infants viewed their caregivers in a frightening way or sensed the caregivers as frightened themselves. Infants approaching their caregivers with fear may have developed this behavior because of distressing or painful experiences in their relationships when the caregivers are supposed to be a consistent source of comfort (such as physical abuse or emotionally hurtful patterns of anger toward the infants). Unsure about whether they should avoid or seek closeness with a parent, these children did not have a strong sense of which adult is safe.

Although the disorganized/disoriented infants were the smallest percentage of the four attachment groups, they demonstrated the most relational challenges with developing a sense of self, which contributed to future challenges in maintaining relationships with others. These mothers were often found to be struggling with unresolved trauma, and the impacts of such disorganized patterns on children experiencing this caregiving style in turn led to disorganized coping skills and increased levels of chronic stress (Spangler & Grossman, 1993). The disorganized attachment model is found in approximately 80% of children associated with high-risk family/home environments associated with trauma and neglect (Siegel, 2013).

Reactive Attachment

Siegel (2013) makes a point to mention a specific case in which a child may not have had opportunities in their early years to experience either secure or insecure attachment due to the unavailability of a consistent caregiver. Thus, their behavior reveals severe challenges with handling emotions and maintaining relationships as a means of coping with a non-existent attachment history. This is known as reactive attachment and is very distinct from the other insecurity models that have been previously discussed. Some common signs of possible reactive attachment include a child who seeks none or minimal comfort from adults when distressed and a history of insufficient care in which social/emotional needs were not met (American Psychiatric Association, 2013). When working to support children with reactive attachment, it is helpful for adults to understand that their children are doing the best they can without secure or insecure attachment experiences. Examples of early environments that may potentially lead to the development of reactive attachment are multiple short-term foster environments or orphanage settings with inconsistent caretakers and/or possible neglect.

Students observed to have this type of intensity with handling emotional regulation in schools may benefit from support through a behavior plan if their behaviors present extreme challenges to functioning in the learning environment. It is necessary to consult with the student's teacher(s), school counselor, school psychologist, administrator, parent/guardian, and other relevant school staff to collaborate on the best way to support the student as they strive to meet academic and/or social-emotional expectations. Just as being informed about trauma can help create emotionally safe climates and more compassionate adults in schools, seeking out appropriate sources such as the school counselor to ensure you are educated and knowledgeable about reactive attachment is best practice when providing support for a student in this context.

SELF-CHECK

Think about your attachment patterns with your parents, teachers, and other caretakers during your childhood. Do you notice any connections between your childhood attachments and the ways you interact in your current relationships?

Complex Trauma

Learning about attachment is essential for understanding how relationships can play a substantial part in the development of trauma, specifically complex trauma. When the adults whom children are supposed to depend on for comfort, protection, and safety become a consistent source of terror from hurtful experiences, these children may struggle with the effects of such stress for extended periods of time and even into adulthood (Spinazzola et al., 2017). Insecure attachment experiences have the potential to develop into complex trauma, as the unpredictability and inconsistency in a caretaker's relationship with a child can cause significant hurt and harm and foster an extremely sensitive amygdala that keeps the brain and body in survival mode. Complex trauma can impact individuals in different ways and is described as early life events that encompass chronic and prolonged encounters with personal or relational adverse experiences (Anda et al., 2006). Some characteristics of complex trauma include its developmental nature, persistence, progressive risk over time, and "a violation of the basic safety and support expected in intimate relationships" (Wolpow, Johnson, Hertel, & Kincaid, 2016, p. 9). It is common for children to hold discomfort with feelings in their bodies from experiencing prolonged stress, and the long-term effects of complex trauma may cause confusion and hopelessness in frustrated older youth when adversity happened in earlier childhood (Spinazzola et al., 2017). Children who struggle with cumulative negative experiences and consistently feel they have no adults to count on or turn to may develop a damaging view of self as a result of accepting blame for unfortunate circumstances and incidents preventing them from basic emotional needs of love and value as a human being (Spinazzola et al., 2017).

Attachment in Schools

The quality of students' attachment to peers and educators influences their capability to engage in learning. When students carry a trauma history, attachment is at the heart of understanding the complexities of relationships and how adults can serve as catalysts toward healing through meaningful connections and experiences. Nonsecure models are important for us to understand, as the knowledge enhances our confidence in approaching students who might be struggling with trauma backgrounds, especially when the trauma has developed or is developing within the context of relationships. We can enhance our curiosity and compassion toward students, colleagues, and ourselves in the context of the meaningful work we do in schools once we begin to understand the possibility that oftentimes, "hurt people *hurt* people" (Romero, Robertson & Warner, 2018, p. 23). Anda (2006) explains that:

> When a child is wounded, the pain and negative long-term effects reverberate as an echo of the lives of people they grew up with—and then they grow up, at risk for taking on the same characteristics and behaviors—thereby sustaining the cycle of abuse, neglect, violence and substance abuse, and mental illness. (p. 14)

We cannot assume that what happens at home is not our problem, since the effects of negative attachment experiences may manifest as the behaviors we observe in students in the classroom.

Instinctively, our social brains as children and adults are wired to connect, learn, belong, and feel valued with a strong desire to be treated with respect and compassion (Cozolino, 2012, 2014). As mentioned in Chapter 1, understanding behavior as communication is at the heart of our work in schools as we strive to provide a trauma-informed learning environment for students who may be suffering from and/or exhibiting behavior stemming from unresolved trauma. When students with trauma can only anticipate dreadful outcomes to typically non-threatening images and situations, their perception of danger could produce an extreme sense of aggression and terror that results in "perplexing" behaviors and responses (van der Kolk, 2014), as teachers and other staff members lack the background information to interpret these behaviors. Caring relationships that are communicated from adults to students through verbal and nonverbal messages are fundamental to establishing a school climate that fosters trust and helps to overcome assumptions that trauma-induced behavior is intentional defiance or disrespect.

It would be impractical to expect that misunderstandings and moments of miscommunication can be completely avoided throughout life. It is also inevitable for busy parents and educators to become distracted and miss opportunities to connect with children. This becomes an issue if young children do not experience reconnection after these minor states of misattunement. Positive, therapeutic moments can consistently be offered to children to strengthen patterned experiences that can outweigh memories of negative interactions (Perry, 1997). For some school staff, feeling overwhelmed by the increasing amount of responsibilities often leads to adults adapting their own behavior to survival mode and automatically switching gears toward a less mindful state. This may be expressed by responding to students harshly, critically, impatiently, and/or dismissively as a swift way of relieving their own stresses. In these cases, educators themselves may be communicating through their behavior the message that they are either stressed in that moment or not well in general. It is only human for adults to feel overwhelmed at times and do the best they can with what they have at the moment to cope with the daily stresses that come with working in a school environment. When we recognize that adults may encounter their own sets of challenges in this way or reflect on our own overwhelming experiences, what might lead someone to think children are immune to having struggles or that children's stressors are less valuable than ours?

Part of being human is the need to feel connected to the people around us and know that we can depend on them for comfort (Seigel, 2013). The crucial thing to remember about these moments is that although we may have acted in a way that ruptured our connections with others, it is up to us to take responsibility for modeling our own regulations and appropriate ways to handle such stresses through intentional repairing of relationships with students. It would be unfair to expect our students to take care of us or be understanding about our own stress when we do not do the same for them, especially when they are still developing those very skills of self-regulation in comparison to our more developed brains and nervous systems. When we miss opportunities to restore relationships with students, we are not taking advantage of our power to shape their neural growth and functioning to optimize development through our attachments with them (Siegel, 2014). After learning about the impact of relationships on brain development in Chapter 2 and the different models of attachment in this chapter,

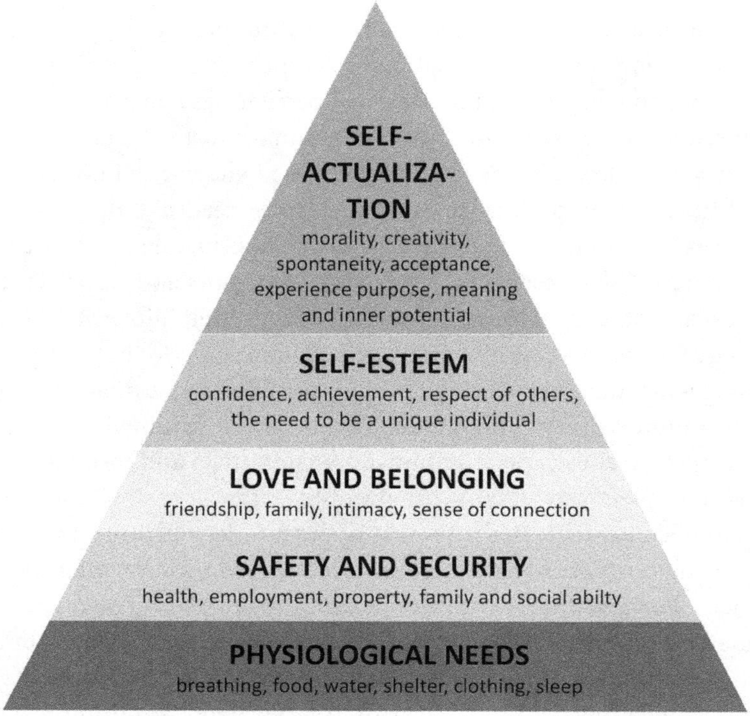
SELF-
ACTUALIZA-
TION
morality, creativity,
spontaneity, acceptance,
experience purpose, meaning
and inner potential
SELF-ESTEEM
confidence, achievement, respect of others,
the need to be a unique individual
LOVE AND BELONGING
friendship, family, intimacy, sense of connection
SAFETY AND SECURITY
health, employment, property, family and social abilty
PHYSIOLOGICAL NEEDS
breathing, food, water, shelter, clothing, sleep

FIGURE 3.1. Maslow's Hierarchy of Needs

imagine what kind of attachment pattern you would be creating with a student if you repaired (or did not repair) moments of potential disconnection with them.

Of course, we would love for each and every one of our students to arrive at school already equipped with the social/emotional tools and resiliency necessary to learn and do exactly what we would like them to do, because it makes our lives easier and helps prove that we are effective educators. This expectation may easily become counterproductive by creating additional stress and anxiety for school staff members who adhere to unrealistic expectations of student academic performance, when the reality is that students may be coming to school with basic physical, emotional, or social needs insufficiently being met at home. You can see from Maslow's Hierarchy of Needs in Figure 3.1 that meeting children's basic needs, such as food, clothing, shelter, and safety are vital for calming their amygdalas and gaining access to their PFCs. Yet there are many children who arrive at school deprived of these very basic things and spend hours at school without relief from toxic stress because a buffering adult may not be available in the building.

There are times when we unconsciously send negative messages to students through our tone, body language, and facial expressions. Although unintentional, the stress this may create for students works against one of our most fundamental goals as educators: to provide a physically and emotionally safe learning environment so that brains are ready for optimal learning. Although unintentional and at times inaccurate, one common message adults can unconsciously communicate to children is that they favor one child over another. Children are aware of what constitutes fairness and pay close attention to our behaviors in order to judge our integrity and level of genuineness (Romero, Robertson, and Warner, 2018). Another hidden message students might receive from adults in the learning environment through seemingly dismissive or impatient attitudes is "I don't care that you have not yet learned the necessary skills—I expect you to figure it out and perform to my expectations without my support because I'm too busy." This message may be conveyed through various ways in different contexts, yet the message received is the same.

For example, a hidden message that may provoke high levels of anxiety for some students is when they experience a teacher who is introducing brand-new content that is challenging and difficult to grasp, and those students do not feel comfortable asking questions due to an impression that the teacher is not approachable or the expectation that the teacher will seem burdened by repeating parts of the lesson again. If we make efforts to maintain an awareness of how our verbal and nonverbal communication might be received by students, relational bonds may begin to be strengthened as students feel more connected and motivated to engage. For students struggling with trauma backgrounds, it is essential for educators to understand that the learning issues related to impaired brain development as a result of toxic stress require our patience with supporting their need for repeated instructions and learning.

Quality of Teacher–Student Relationships

Since our brains are social organs and we learn best in the context of meaningful relationships, we naturally learn best from educators who demonstrate compassion and care for students (Cozolino, 2014). Teacher–student connections are just as important as academic content, and because attachment enhances learning, we can no longer view the two in isolation from each other if the goal is student success. Howes and Ritchie (2002) explain, "When child–teacher attachment relationships are secure, children trust that they can get help from their teacher when they need it" (p. 13). Establishing secure attachment with students in the classroom is especially necessary for those who exhibit learning challenges due to histories of trauma.

When students come to school with poor neural wiring because their needs were not met in earlier experiences, it is important for the adults in the school environment to be aware of actions that may send reinforcing messages of "I'm not willing to support you" when students ask for help. Helping students should not be misunderstood as "enabling" or "giving in" if they have not yet developed the cognitive and emotional skills necessary to meet our expectations; simply meeting them where they are communicates care, respect, and willingness to understand students' experiences. It is possible and appropriate to hold them accountable for realistic expectations when it is balanced with an appropriate level of support (Evans & Vaandering, 2016). It is also sometimes helpful to step back and see the big picture, as educators often get consumed into heavy left-brain modes throughout the extremely busy school day. Successful student learning is the heart of what we strive to accomplish every day in schools, and unfortunately, a common rationale for some educators is: *Since students are not learning based on my teaching methods and the assessments, the student is flawed.*

When students are unable to experience the four Ss of attachment, both at home and school, think about what kind of impact this might have on their neural and emotional development. The reality of what we are faced with today is that we cannot control the negative experiences some students may carry with them as they enter school day after day. What we *can* control is our awareness and intention to become secure attachment figures to help provide opportunities for students to encounter a safe harbor if they have not yet had the chance or have not had enough experiences to feel cared for before stepping into school. For other students, our interactions can continue to serve as reinforcing ways to help strengthen the neural networks already in place that allow for healthy coping and resiliency in the face of challenges. Cozolino (2014) states:

> The position of the teacher parallels that of a parent in building a child's brain. Both can support emotional regulation by providing a safe haven that supports the learning process. This support, balanced with an appropriate level of challenge, activates the proper balance of neurotransmitters to create the states of mind and brain that activate memory and learning.
>
> Teacher–student attunement is especially important with at-risk students. The social brain takes into account what we are learning and whom we are learning it from. Teachers can provide safe, trusting relationships by addressing shame, increasing independence, and strengthening bonds. (p. 36)

Offering secure attachment relationships to students can be beneficial for future success in becoming capable and passionate learners.

Siegel (2013) reminds us that some of the challenges faced particularly by adolescents that are related to mental health, such as drug abuse/addiction or anxiety and mood disorders, may be attributed to the remodeling phase of neural development and may not necessarily be caused by attachment issues. Serious clinical issues like these can develop for an individual who has experienced secure attachment, as other variables (social relationships, temperament, genetics, socioeconomic status, and substance use/abuse) may influence the progression of such conditions. Additionally, Sroufe's (2005) study acknowledges that:

> While it is not proper to think of attachment variations as directly causing certain out-comes, and while early attachment has no privileged causal status, it is nonetheless the case that nothing can be assessed in infancy that is more important. Infant attachment is critical, both because of its place in initiating pathways of development and because of its connection with so many critical developmental functions—social relatedness, arousal modulation, emotional regulation, and curiosity, to name just a few. Attachment experiences remain, even in this complex view, vital in the formation of the person. (p. 365)

Social Environments

Attachment patterns continue throughout our entire lives, with friends, partners, co-workers, social relationships, relatives, etc. An individual can have different attachment responses with different people in their lives, based on which model is triggered in a certain situation. For example, you might have a best friend in whom you feel safe enough to confide anything, even things that are embarrassing for you to share. You feel a strong sense that they will listen and support you without judgment. You willingly spend your time engaging in this mutually rewarding friendship in which you feel heard and understood, and your internal sense of feeling good and safe in a trusting relationship leads you to form a secure attachment with that friend. When you experience stressful situations, you seek out this friend because you can count on them to be your safe haven. You have developed an internal sense that you will consistently be welcomed to share your vulnerable moments and that you will be comforted by their presence and understanding of your experiences.

Additionally, at your workplace you might intentionally avoid a co-worker or supervisor because you expect to receive negative feedback or be treated disrespectfully, as is usually the case based on the majority of experiences interacting with this individual. These experiences might leave you feeling underappreciated with a deflated sense of self-worth for not being seen or recognized for any of your positive attributes or contributions to the workplace. You would rather hear nothing at all instead of criticism, so you strategically steer clear from any possibility of being in their presence. (Or you might become an employee whose stress leads to productivity issues or many sick days—not much different, in a sense, from students who cannot learn or skip school!) Interacting with this individual causes such distress that your method of coping is to purposely avoid any chance of being around them, thus sparing yourself from potential emotional hurt.

These are only examples of what secure and insecure adult relationships might look like. Based on an individual's level of resiliency and self-awareness, an insecure adult relationship may sustain enough negative patterns of interactions to cause significant distress. For individuals with a history of unresolved interpersonal trauma, the intensity and impact of negative interactions within a potential relationship may result in sensations that become triggers for retraumatization (van der Kolk, 2014). Sensations like these may arise from early attachment experiences of shame that are stored as painful memories, such as feeling disconnected, excluded, or abandoned. The impact of such harmful experiences may cause an individual to inevitably expect that future social interactions will be destructive, thus negatively shaping one's behavior and thoughts about the self and others.

Practice #1

Often the "Do as I say, not as I do" mentality is embedded in the day-to-day messages from adults in schools through our interactions and expectations of students. Though we may not notice it ourselves, many students focus on what we say and our actions to determine whether we are genuine, trustworthy, and dependable. They may even test us at times and at length to observe whether we stay true to our word and model what we preach because that reveals authenticity.

Below are examples of some things school staff members might do in the presence of students. Take a few minutes to reflect on what each behavior might be modeling for students:

- Pulling a student aside and calmly asking if they are feeling okay
- Gossiping with another teacher about co-workers and/or students in front of other students
- Yelling at students to be quiet as you walk down the hallway
- Saying "Hello" to each student you encounter in the morning before school starts
- Keeping students in your classroom when the lunch period begins to finish a test and then eating your own lunch at your desk while you wait for them to finish
- Picking up random trash in common areas as you walk by
- Sitting next to a co-worker and socializing during a guest speaker presentation to students
- Showing your co-worker a picture on your phone and criticizing or putting down someone in the picture in the presence of students

Shame

The concept of shame may sometimes be confused with guilt, but they do not hold the same meanings. **Shame** is associated with a strong and painful feeling that you are essentially flawed and unworthy, while **guilt** is characterized by a feeling of psychological discomfort about something wrong we did that violated objective principles of moral behavior (National Institute for the Clinical Application of Behavioral Medicine, 2017). The concept of "tough love" may sometimes become inaccurately translated into the belief that in order for children to learn, they need to hurt. Consequences and consistency are not synonymous with corporal punishment. Whether it be physical or emotional pain, purposely shaming a child as a method of discipline has damaging effects on their development of emotional regulation and self-worth (Schore & Schore, 2008). Experiences of shame cause the physical body and brain to shut down, and the stress associated with shame hinders neuroplasticity that is necessary for novelty and fresh learning.

When a young child anticipates sharing happiness or excitement with a caretaker and receives negative responses, such as disapproval, anger, or apathy, perpetually hurtful experiences of disconnection can create feelings of shame and rejection that may evolve into anxiousness or sensitivity in situations that appear to be ordinary (Cozolino, 2013). The same can happen in the classroom between a teacher/school staff member and a student. Just as conscientious parents try to repair disconnection with a child promptly afterwards to prevent shameful experiences, educators can similarly provide intentional opportunities for reattunement with students after possible ruptures in the relationships to reduce the possibility of creating or reinforcing an internal sense of low self-worth in the students. This requires the educator to demonstrate a certain level of self-awareness that allows for open-mindedness and curiosity about a student's previous experiences, as opposed to feeling defensive and resentful.

In *Attachment-Based Teaching* (2013), Louis Cozolino describes core shame as "the experience of being fundamentally defective, worthless, and unlovable as a human being." He emphasizes the difference between core shame and appropriate shame, in which the latter equates to selfish or careless behavior that has violated the principles of a community and can be turned into social/emotional learning opportunities. Concepts of self-esteem and core shame are typically encoded into the unconscious at an early age through attachment experiences, and the trauma a young child experiences from losing a parent or caretaker due to events such as incarceration, divorce, or death may be understood as rejection. A student with a trauma background who experiences school and learning as endless failure may adapt to shutting down as a coping mechanism for avoiding the shame and embarrassment that is expected to follow. This type of response may negatively impact a student's academic performance, as the terror of uncertainty that comes with exploration and creativity creates a high level of anxiety that hinders new learning.

Core shame may develop from circumstances such as mismatched personalities or temperaments between parents and children or parents with childhood histories of neglect, abandonment, or abuse who adopt parenting styles characterized by harsh criticism and unwarranted shaming. This can have long-term devastating effects on a child's psyche and capacity for building healthy relationships, as it may lead to fear and anxiety about taking reasonable risks in typical situations due to distorted expectations of failure, rejection, criticism and isolation. One of the biggest challenges for individuals who experience trauma from abuse is that they often blame themselves for what happened to them despite their lack of control in those situations. They learn to accept that they are "defective" and are the problem, justifying the "deserved" abuse by the perpetrators.

When students with core shame enter our schools, the coping mechanisms they have learned to develop to protect themselves from enduring more potential hurt become barriers to new learning, since every opportunity to learn comes with the risk of failure or making mistakes. When given constructive feedback for earning less than perfect scores, a student's amygdala may go into overdrive as they struggle to deal with the fact that they made any errors. Some unfortunate outcomes of such extreme anxiety and fear may emerge as an inability to take in new information, lack of curiosity to explore new ideas and optimize creativity, and lack of flexibility in working toward solving problems.

Individuals with core shame may also perceive experiences of minor abandonment as threats to survival. For example, middle school and older elementary students with core shame may display severe and intense emotional difficulties as a response to ruptures in friendships while becoming hypersensitive to feelings of exclusion or rejection when sensing that peers are upset with or ignoring them. This social dynamic can become so easily toxic and unhealthy when conflicts are frequent within the same circle of friends, and especially when members of the same social group are not learning or making progress on how to improve communication styles. In cases like these, students can be affected by **vicarious** or **secondary trauma**, in which empathy for another individual's traumatic pain or suffering leads to personal upset and internalization of upsetting incidents that are not personally experienced (Wolpow, Johnson, Hertel, & Kincaid, 2016). Students may experience vicarious trauma in the form of peer-to-peer or adult-to-peer, which is why it is so important for school staff members to maintain awareness of how their interactions might be affecting students. Adults in schools have a collective responsibility for supporting and guiding students through challenging relational conflicts, and overlooking the advantages of this influential role would be a missed learning opportunity for the staff to work toward secure and healthy relationships with students and each other.

Practice #2

To help you review what you have learned in this chapter, complete the chart below with basic descriptions that characterize the different attachment models. This exercise can be done individually or with a partner.

Attachment Model	Early Caretaker Experiences	Common Behaviors/ Responses of Child	Message Child Is Communicating
Secure			
Avoidant			
Anxious/ Ambivalent			
Disorganized			
Reactive Attachment			

Once you have finished, continue to add relevant information as you learn more about attachment models while gaining work experience in schools. It can be printed out and kept in a convenient place as a "cheat sheet" to practice reflecting on what a student's behavior might be communicating in their interaction with you, a peer, or a colleague. Keep in mind that having a history of a certain attachment model does not automatically define or predict a set of outcomes for any one person. It serves as a resource and guide for reflecting on how behavior is communication. Practicing positive communication and modeling respect and compassion contribute to development of an open mind about interactions within relationships through a trauma-informed lens.

Practice #3

The following chart contains examples of potentially harmful statements that might be used by school faculty and staff in response to various student behaviors, both inside and outside the classroom in the course of a school day. Although it is not the intention, these simple statements on the left (or similar) can be possible triggers for students with trauma histories, especially when the trauma is related to early experiences of shame. Examples of possible interpretations of such statements are given in the table on the next page in bold italics. An alternative trauma-informed response is provided in the right column, which uses language that communicates absence of judgment and a willingness to support the student. Take a moment to also consider the potential body language for each corresponding column of statements. Expressing positive verbal comments alone is not enough if the energy of one's tone and body language appear misaligned.

Keep in mind that these are examples and that the skill of communicating these messages positively is based on your own personality and style as an educator or support staff in the school environment. Several different adults can recite the same words or teach the same lesson to a group of students, yet the nature of how it is delivered is what determines whether attunement takes place. The benefits of setting a warm and accepting tone include building trust and keeping your relationships with students genuine. As mentioned earlier, use of a condescending tone, judgmental facial expression, and/or negative body language in conjunction with positive statements only validates the message those students receive through feelings—that they are not worthy of our time and energy to stop and consider what might be going on with them.

Read the first three examples below. Then try to create your own trauma-informed approaches for the next three statements (you may refer back to Figure 1.2 in Chapter 1 to help conceptualize your responses). Share your statements with a partner and take turns discussing how you might personally receive their trauma-informed statements. Use this exercise to expand your ideas about how you can practice purposeful language to communicate care, respect, and compassion toward students.

Now think about your earlier experiences in school or other environments where adults were responsible for you. Write down three statements describing situations in which you or someone you know may have been addressed by an adult in a way that felt offensive or disrespectful, possibly causing feelings of disconnection.

Statements/Assumptions	Trauma-Informed Approach
It's not a big deal. **(Shows lack of empathy/care/compassion in the moment for what student may be experiencing and communicates an unwillingness to understand.)**	*I can see that this is a big deal to you. Could you explain what happened so I can understand what made you frustrated?*
I already gave instructions, so you weren't listening. Figure it out. **(Assumes every student learns in the same way and has the necessary skills to successfully process material presented by the teacher's teaching style.)**	*Maybe I wasn't clear enough when I explained it earlier. Let me try and explain it again, and you can let me know if you still don't understand.*
You should know what to do because I said it twice already. You need to listen. **(Assumes that since the student does not know what to do, they purposely did not listen to instructions. If the student was listening but did not understand, then the student is flawed.)**	*It seems there might be something you're confused about. Let me help you get started so I can answer any questions you may have.*
This is my classroom, and all of you need to show respect by cleaning up.	
Stop being dramatic and just get over it.	
You're refusing to do the work, since you didn't turn in your homework.	

There may be some students who have developed enough emotional resiliency to shrug these comments off and be okay with continuing on with their days without any ruptures in relationships with adults. This does not indicate that they are "better" or worthier of our attention than their peers who may be more sensitive and lack the neural integration necessary for appropriate self-regulation. It is impossible to accurately predict which students will be triggered at any time, and to assume so may produce barriers to progress in shifting one's paradigm toward a trauma-informed approach.

CASE EXAMPLE #1

Mrs. Smith is a fifth-grade teacher with a class of 26 students. Unless Mrs. Smith is actively teaching a lesson using the whiteboard or Activboard, she spends most of class time sitting in her chair behind her desk and addressing students from that physical location. One day after administering a math test to the class, Mrs. Smith asks the students to randomly switch their tests with classmates and take out red pens for correcting the tests together as a group while Mrs. Smith reads aloud the 20 answers. After they finish correcting aloud, Mrs. Smith instructs students to indicate how many answers were marked incorrect by writing minus signs and the numbers wrong with their red pens at the top of the first pages. Students are then asked to return the corrected tests to the owners and then return to their seats. Mrs. Smith then says to the class:

"Let's see how everyone did on the test.
Raise your hand if you got none wrong.
Raise your hand if you got two wrong.
Raise your hand if you got three wrong.
Raise your hand if you got four wrong.
Raise your hand if you got five wrong.
Raise your hand if you got six wrong."

At this point, everyone in the class has raised their hands in response to the corresponding number of answers wrong on their tests, except for one student. Mrs. Smith, who continues to periodically glance at her cell phone on her desk, continues addressing the class:

"Raise your hand if you got seven wrong.
Raise your hand if you got eight wrong."

Carlos raises his hand while he looks down at his desk and sits with a hunched-over posture. Carlos is a native Spanish speaker, and it is the primary language spoken at home. He is able to communicate with peers successfully in English and does not meet the qualifications for ELL services based on his assessments for English language skills. Mrs. Smith looks up from her phone and says, "If you got more than eight wrong, you didn't pass the test and you need to do a better job next time." Carlos proceeds to put his head down on his desk and stare out the window. He uses his pencil to write the following on his test:

I'm stupid

FIGURE 3.2.

As Mrs. Smith transitions the class to start the science period, Carlos remains in the same position with his head down. He does not engage in the next class lesson.

DISCUSSION QUESTIONS

1. What are your initial thoughts about Carlos's behavior after the tests were corrected?
2. What did you learn in this chapter that may have helped you develop a more attuned understanding about what Carlos's behavior might be communicating?
3. What are some things you noticed about Mrs. Smith's classroom climate that might contribute to a lack of attunement with students?
4. After noticing Carlos's behavior and what he wrote about himself, how might you respond using a trauma-informed approach?

CASE EXAMPLE #2

Sean is a third-grade student who is currently living with foster parents and has been living with them for the past year. Sean has a trauma history of neglect and abuse by his biological mother, and he has not known his father since birth. The public school he attends has been collaborating with Sean's foster parents closely to make sure Sean is properly supported when he encounters any academic or behavioral difficulties. Although there are times when Sean becomes highly dysregulated and his behavior becomes a challenge during the school day, his educational support team provides a consistently high level of care and patience that is similar to what Sean receives from his foster parents. The foster parents have done their best to provide a safe, calm, and nurturing home environment filled with unconditional care and have started the process of trying to adopt Sean.

Sean's biological parents are of African American descent, his foster mother's ethnicity is Asian, and his foster father's ethnicity is Caucasian. The school counselor helps to support Sean with processing his experiences regarding various transitions, including making sense of his identity, since Sean often mentions how different he looks from his foster parents. The school counselor notices how Sean holds a curious and lengthy gaze toward Mr. Hill, a first-grade instructional assistant, whenever they pass each other in the hallway. Mr. Hill is the only African American staff member in the entire school, and Sean often asks his counselor curious and random questions about Mr. Hill. The school counselor consults with Mr. Hill confidentially and asks Mr. Hill if he would mind greeting Sean in the mornings, since Sean seems to be interested in who he is. Mr. Hill begins to intentionally seek out Sean every morning before school starts to take a few minutes to chat with Sean, and they instantly develop a positive connection. One month later at the next IEP meeting, Sean's IEP team shares their observations of how Sean seems enthusiastic about coming to school lately and that Sean happily volunteers to briefly help Mr. Hill set up his first-grade classroom before school starts.

DISCUSSION QUESTIONS

1. How could student relationships with faculty and support staff like Mr. Hill (instructional assistants, bus drivers, cafeteria or maintenance employees, etc.) benefit students with trauma histories?
2. Do you think the counselor's consultation with Mr. Hill was in Sean's best interests?
3. If you were a participant in Sean's IEP team meeting as a teacher, school counselor, or administrator, what other questions or information would you seek out to discuss Sean's progress?

Chapter Summary

Attachment is at the heart of understanding the complexities of relationships, as it significantly shapes our sense of self and how we relate to the world and others around us. Our continued learning on this topic provides a basis for how we can serve as catalysts for our students by providing healing experiences that lead to positive neural wiring so learning can occur. It is important to understand a basic level of infant attachment because infants' experiences of relational patterns with their caregiver(s) have an astounding impact on early periods of brain development. This early hardwiring establishes strong neural networks in which relationship patterns are carried over into adolescence and adulthood and may develop into complex trauma. Complex trauma may potentially harm healthy development and can serve as an unrecognized source of issues challenging older youth and adults.

Knowledge about secure and nonsecure attachment models in the context of trauma-informed practices is not meant to suggest that this knowledge be used to make swift assumptions and immediately categorize students into a box based on observations of their behavior. Adding knowledge of attachment models to our trauma lens increases our confidence in feeling that we are better equipped in schools to have the patience and flexibility to handle the unexpected daily challenges that continue to rise. We can help restore children's capacity for secure attachment by offering positive and meaningful moments through our relationships with them.

It is possible to have more than one attachment style with different individuals, thus implying the value of adults in schools remaining patient, grounded, and open-minded about potential triggers and needs of students. These learned models serve as a context for how we can begin to successfully reverse the effects of insecure attachment models and enhance secure models for our students through consistent, predictable, and soothing ways of interacting in the classroom and school in general.

Connect and Reflect

Take some time to think about your own attachment history with your parent(s)/caretaker(s) during childhood. Use the following questions to begin reflecting on what you notice about your attachment style(s):

> *What was your attachment style like growing up?*
> *Did you have different styles with different adults in your life?*
> *Was there at least one person you always felt safe with? If so, what are some of their qualities that contributed to your sense of feeling safe?*
> *Was there a particular person who helped you feel calm just by being in their presence?*
> *What specific qualities did they possess that helped make you feel safe?*

Now reflect on how your previous patterns may have impacted your current style of relationships with various people:

> *Siblings*
> *Friends*
> *Spouse/Partner*
> *Co-worker/Supervisor*
> *Your own children*
> *Mentors*
> *Professors*
> *Other(s)*

Making sense of how our attachment histories impact past, current, and future interactions with others will begin to help us to intentionally shift away from insecure attachments toward a more secure model (Siegel, 2013). An added benefit is that maintaining awareness of our attachment patterns as we navigate through relationships in our work and personal lives can help empower us with confidence that we are emotionally equipped to take care of our students, especially during challenging moments.

Extended Learning

Cozolino, L. (2014). *Attachment-based teaching: Creating a tribal classroom.* New York, NY: W.W. Norton & Company.

Howes, C., & Ritchie, S. (2002). *A matter of trust: Connecting teachers and learners in the early childhood classroom.* New York, NY: Teachers College Press.

Siegel, D. J. (2015). *Brainstorm: The power and purpose of the teenage brain.* New York, NY: Jeremy P. Tarcher/Penguin.

Siegel, D. J., & Hartzell, M. (2014). *Parenting from the inside out: How a deeper self-understanding can help you raise children who thrive* (10th anniversary ed.). New York, NY: Jeremy P. Tarcher/Penguin.

Credit

Chapter 4

Adverse Childhood Experiences (ACEs)

Aᴅᴠᴇʀsᴇ ᴄʜɪʟᴅʜᴏᴏᴅ ᴇxᴘᴇʀɪᴇɴᴄᴇs (ACEs) are becoming more commonly recognized as *the new normal* for students in the classroom, especially for individuals who have recently stepped into the profession to begin their careers in education settings ranging from early learning through high school levels (Romero, Robertson, & Warner, 2018). Much research has revealed that ACEs are common, interrelated, and wield a cumulative effect in which one isolated ACE for an individual's history is seldom the case and signals necessary consideration for additional exposures to ACEs (Chapman, Dube, & Anda, 2007).

It is essential for school leadership teams to understand the value of educating school personnel about ACEs and trauma due to the alarming outcomes related to student learning, functioning, and well-being. Learning about trauma alone or in isolation is not enough to understand or tackle the wide array of student behaviors stemming from childhood adversity (Perry, 2009). Investing in the well-being of students through positive, respectful, and caring interpersonal relationships can serve as a protective barrier for all students who may be experiencing high levels of toxic stress and adversity that can help promote healing and model a culture of safety within healthy school environments. Without awareness of the harmful effects of trauma and ACEs on children's health and developmental systems, learning communities are faced with missed opportunities to provide necessary support and professional development that would help alleviate the rising levels of stress driving talented educators toward burnout or the desire to leave the profession altogether.

Learning Objectives

1. What is the ACE Study?
2. What are the 10 types of childhood trauma the ACE survey addresses?
3. What are some additional ACEs not included in the survey?
4. What are the impacts of ACEs and trauma on student behavior?
5. How do the three types of stress-response systems differ?

ACE Study

The Adverse Childhood Experiences (ACEs) Study, published in 1998, was led by Vincent Felitti from Kaiser Permanente and Robert Anda from the Centers for Disease Control and Prevention (CDC). Nadine Burke Harris (2018) thoroughly describes how this study made a significant contribution to the medical field and developed as a result of a mistake in standard questioning of a patient by Felitti in an obesity clinic in San Diego in 1985. Felitti was perplexed about the program's dropout rate of some of his most successful patients after working persistently to reach their weight goals. Some patients had permanently left the program, while others returned later after regaining the weight they were previously successful in losing while attending the clinic.

In his efforts to obtain a better understanding of what could be possibly causing these outcomes, Felitti administered a set of standard questions to these patients. Due to an unintentional error in questioning, this was the first time Felitti had listened to a patient disclose any experiences related to sexual abuse. This sparked the beginning of Felitti's curiosity about a potential connection between experiences of childhood abuse and obesity. Felitti was later introduced to Anda at the CDC, who had been researching correlations between behavioral health and cardiovascular disease. Together, their pioneering research evolved into a large-scale study from 1995–1997 that is widely known today as the ACE Study (Felitti et al., 1998), in which adverse childhood experiences were identified and compared with adult health risk behavior and disease.

More than 17,000 adult health plan members of Kaiser Permanente in San Diego, California, agreed to participate in the ACE Study and received surveys in the mail following their standard medical visits to the clinic between 1995 and 1997. This confidential questionnaire inquired about each patient's childhood experiences related to abuse and other types of household dysfunction before the age of eighteen and also included questions about current health risk factors, such as smoking, substance abuse, depressed moods, etc. This study "found a strong relationship between the number of childhood exposures and the number of health risk factors for leading causes of death in adults" (Felitti et al., 1998, p. 250). One significant component of the data revealed that a majority of the participants were Caucasian, middle class, college educated, and medically insured through Kaiser Permanente. This enlightens us to the fact that despite any previous assumptions we may have had about trauma, any individual has the capacity to experience trauma regardless of ethnicity, socioeconomic status, religion, gender, etc. Trauma does not discriminate.

Dr. Nadine Burke Harris, California's first appointed and current surgeon general since January 2019 and founder of the Center for Youth Wellness in Bayview, California, is an active leader in the movement to raise global awareness about the impact of ACEs. In her work leading up to significant contributions to the field, Harris analyzed her own patient files of children referred for behavior problems and found an overwhelming connection revealing that these children were experiencing toxic doses of adversity (Burke Harris, 2018). The alarming difference between the original ACE Study and Burke's data is that the mean age of patients in the ACE Study was 55, while the mean age for Burke's patients was 8. Burke's patients had not completed accumulation of ACEs since they had not reached the age of 18 yet, leaving much room for potentially higher ACE scores by the time they become adults.

The ACE Study additionally highlights how a shift toward acceptance of asking about early childhood trauma would be helpful in understanding risk factors contributing to behavioral, academic, and social emotional challenges for students (Edwards, Dube, Felitti, & Anda, 2007). Risks associated with cumulative ACEs have increased negative consequences on an individual's health, as a single ACE can contribute to additional risks (Felitti et al., 1998; Larkin, Felitti, & Anda, 2013). A study supported by the CDC and conducted by Finkelhor, Turner, Ormrod, Hamby, and Kracke (2009) "clearly illustrates the cumulative effects on children exposed to multiple incidents of violence and how exposure to one form of violence may make a child more vulnerable to other forms" (p. 8). Collaboration among leadership staff is necessary to ensure that any process of obtaining such information from students maintains best practices and is done professionally in a manner that maintains the privacy and dignity of the child and family and includes cultural considerations.

Types of Childhood Trauma

The ACE Study focused on 10 types of childhood trauma that were the most common among participants who completed the survey. The ACE survey aimed to determine each participant's frequency of exposure to adverse childhood experiences using the following three identified categories, accounting for one point per subcategory with a total of 10 possible points:

Abuse

- Emotional (a parent, stepparent, or adult living in your home humiliated, intimidated, used verbal insults, cursed, or engaged in any other actions having a negative impact on your dignity)
- Physical (pushed, grabbed, slapped, hit, threw something at you, left marks or injury)
- Sexual (an adult, relative, family friend, or stranger raped, touched/fondled in a sexual way or made you perform such acts, exposed naked private parts, or attempted to have sexual intercourse)

Household Challenges

- Substance abuse in household (household member was addicted to drugs or alcohol)
- Mental illness in household (household member was depressed, mentally ill, or attempted suicide)
- Domestic violence (any household member was pushed, grabbed, slapped, kicked, hit, bitten, had something thrown at them, threatened or hurt by knife/gun, whether it was adult to adult, adult to child, or child to child)
- Divorce or parental separation (high tension/conflicts between parents)
- Incarcerated family member (household member went to prison)

Neglect

- Emotional (your family did not support each other and/or you did not feel special, loved, or cared for)
- Physical (without adequate food, sleep, hygiene, medical care, supervision, or protection from dangers, or exposure to unsafe situations)

The data from two waves of patient responses found a strong relationship between childhood exposure to adverse experiences and the number of health risk factors for primary causes of death in adults. This means the impact of cumulative and frequent negative childhood experiences produces traumatic stress, anxiety, anger, and depression for children that could manifest into health risk behaviors and diseases into adulthood (Felitti et al., 1998). 59.3% of ACE Study participants who had at least one traumatic childhood experience also reported at least one additional ACE category (Edwards, Dube, Felitti, & Anda, 2007). Events characterized by ACEs serve as risk factors for later development of physical and mental health issues, including altered brain function, suicidality, and resistance to treatment (Chapman, Dube, & Anda, 2007). There are several types of other trauma that exist, such as poverty, which is now considered an additional ACE that is not included in the ACE survey (Hughes, 2018). Other types that are being considered include community violence, homelessness, discrimination, foster care, bullying, repeated medical procedures, life-threatening illnesses, death of a caregiver, loss of a caregiver due to deportation or migration, verbal or physical violence from a romantic partner, and youth incarceration (Burke Harris, 2018).

A meta-analysis on ACEs was later conducted that revealed global data from more than 20 countries with similar results to the original ACE Study, confirming the universal prevalence of ACEs and the significantly higher risk of individuals with four or more ACEs in comparison to those with zero ACEs, noting the influence of the **dose-response** relationship (Hughes et al., 2017). A dose-response relationship means that as an individual's ACE score increases, so does the risk for health problems and disease into adulthood. While ACEs indicate a profoundly increased risk for seven out of 10 leading causes of death in the United States, the increased risk is six out of 10 on a global level (CDC, 2016). The recognition of ACEs as a public health crisis continues to rise internationally, as Scotland is currently leading the movement to establish itself as the first ACE Aware Nation in the world by raising awareness on a national level and prioritizing urgency about ACEs outcomes and prevention (ACE-Aware Scotland, 2019).

Toxic Stress on the Developing Brain

The ACE score appears to be a robust measure of the cumulative lifetime impact of traumatic stress on neurodevelopment in childhood. Stressful and traumatic childhood and adolescent experiences literally become biology, affecting brain structure and functions and thus leading to persistent effects (Anda, n. d.). ACEs have the capacity to negatively impact several developmental systems of a child (Charmandari, 2005; Dube et al., 2009; Ulrich-Lai, 2009). Frequent and prolonged exposure to ACEs causes a child's biological response to be triggered so incessantly that the "over-activation of the stress response affects just about every system in a child's developing brain and body" (Burke Harris, 2019). We learned in Chapter 2 that the body's alert system scans for danger and uses the amygdala to automatically take control over the PFC. In cases where the body's ability to adapt into survival mode becomes continuous and excessive, the stress-response system is altered into a maladaptive state that becomes extremely damaging to an individual's physiological and mental health (Charmandari, Tsigos, & Chrousos, 2005; McEwen & Gianaros, 2010; Ulrich-Lai, 2009).

Activation of the body's stress-response system helps an individual adapt and survive through potentially threatening experiences, resulting in behavioral and physical changes that include heightened arousal, alertness, and vigilance (Charmandari, Tsigos, & Chrousos, 2005). Overstimulated stress responses from toxic doses of adversity may inhibit a student's executive functioning, affecting behavior in the learning environment as well as outside school. Romero, Robertson, and Warner (2018) explain that "ACE students can be prone to reactivity and emotional outbursts that further inhibit their learning while also negatively impacting their relationships with adults and peers" (p. 67). Specifically pertaining to student behaviors and learning in the classroom, the neurological impacts include:

- Long-term alterations to a child's fight/flight response
- Overstimulated fear-response system
- Altered brain structure and functioning that interferes with learning
- Changes to brain biology, including the reward center of the brain, that may result in increased likelihood of addictive/risky behaviors, as indicated in Figure 4.1

Alterations to a child's response system can include struggles with coping when faced with stressors, proneness to reactivity, "acting out" behaviors, and limited emotional development and self-awareness. An overstimulated fear-response system may manifest as emotional outbursts, difficulty managing emotions, and demanding high expectations of others. Changes in neural development due to ACEs can have damaging effects on brain structure and functioning, which can lead to increased risk of dangerous behaviors with potentially serious consequences for adolescents (Finkelhor, 2009). As an attempt to cope with the accumulation of these challenges, individuals may seek relief in risky decisions that could later develop into addictive behaviors. For example, the use of nicotine by early teens may be initially used as a coping mechanism for mood regulation and develop later into addiction (Felitti et al., 1998). As we learned in Chapter 1, teenagers in particular often face disciplinary consequences at school, such as suspensions or expulsions, when they engage in such risky behaviors (Cole et al., 2005).

Frequent experiences of childhood adversity may cause a child's brain to seek higher levels of pleasure from activities than it typically would in the absence of adverse experiences. A neurotransmitter called **dopamine** is associated with the production and adjustment of pleasurable feelings that feel good to us. A release of dopamine is activated during experiences of gratification or enjoyment, such as connecting with friends who nurture your well-being, eating one of your favorite foods, playing a fun game or sport, spending time with your dog, and completing a challenging project or task. An adequate level of dopamine allows us to sustain motivation, delay gratification, and maintain an optimistic perspective on life. Siegel (2013) explains how dopamine is responsible for the brain's desire for reward, and heightened dopamine release, especially during adolescence, can result in impulsiveness and higher vulnerability to addictive behaviors. The dopamine reward part of the brain can become so strong during teen years that the increased drive for satisfaction could lead to addictive cycles despite a child's understanding of its harmful impacts.

Understanding that toxic stress is not the stressor is essential, as toxic stress signifies the actual long-term changes in brain architecture, immune and hormonal systems, and genetic regulation that result in increased risk for long-term health issues and cognitive impairment (Burke Harris, 2019). We previously learned in Chapter 1 that trauma is the process that results from an individual experiencing certain events or circumstances as harmful or life-threatening, creating lasting adverse effects on functioning. An individual's response to such traumatic experiences can diminish capacity for coping with the stress associated with the event or incident (Cole et al., 2005). High levels of toxic stress from traumatic experiences can negatively influence how our body's internal systems react, especially the stress-response system.

ACE Survey

The following survey was developed from the ACE Study (Felitti et al., 1998) and includes a point-scoring system to help determine an individual's ACE score. Take a moment to review the questions, and then take the survey to determine your own ACE score.

ADVERSE CHILDHOOD EXPERIENCES (ACE) QUESTIONNAIRE

Before you turned the age of 18:

1. Did a parent or other adult in the household **often** ...

    Swear at you, insult you, put you down, or humiliate you?

    or

    Act in a way that made you afraid that you might be physically hurt?

    Yes   No   If yes, enter 1 _____

2. Did a parent or other adult in the household **often** ...

    Push, grab, slap, or throw something at you?

    or

    Ever hit you so hard that you had marks or were injured?

    Yes   No   If yes, enter 1 _____

3. Did an adult or person at least 5 years older than you **ever** ...

    Touch or fondle you or have you touch their body in a sexual way?

    or

    Try to actually have oral, anal, or vaginal sex with you?

    Yes   No   If yes, enter 1 _____

4. Did you **often** feel that ...

    No one in your family loved you or thought you were important or special?

    or

    Your family didn't look out for each other, feel close to each other, or support each other?

    Yes   No   If yes, enter 1 _____

5. Did you **often** feel that ...

    You didn't have enough to eat, had to wear dirty clothes, and had no one to protect you?

    or

    Your parents were too drunk or high to take care of you or take you to the doctor if you needed it?

    Yes   No   If yes, enter 1 _____

6. Were your parents **ever** separated or divorced?

   Yes   No   If yes, enter 1 _____

7. Was your mother or stepmother:

   Often pushed, grabbed, slapped, or had something thrown at her?

   or

   Sometimes or often kicked, bitten, hit with a fist, or hit with something hard?

   or

   Ever repeatedly hit over at least a few minutes or threatened with a gun or knife?

   Yes   No   If yes, enter 1 _____

8. Did you live with anyone who was a problem drinker or alcoholic or who used street drugs?

   Yes   No   If yes, enter 1 _____

9. Was a household member depressed or mentally ill, or did a household member attempt suicide?

   Yes   No   If yes, enter 1 _____

10. Did a household member go to prison?

    Yes   No   If yes, enter 1 _____

Now add up your "Yes" answers: _____   ***This is your ACE Score***

An individual's ACE score reflects the risk for future health, social, and emotional issues. A higher ACE score suggests a higher risk of chronic disease and mental health concerns, such as anxiety, depression, and suicide (Felitti et al., 1998; Hughes et al., 2017). An ACE score of four or more was linked to significantly higher risks for negative health outcomes (Hughes et al., 2017). Take a moment to review Figure 4.1. Compared to a person with an ACE score of zero, the following chart indicates health risks associated with various ACE scores.

How would you feel and react if your physician asked you to complete an ACE survey during a routine physical examination? Would you react differently if you had never heard about ACEs before?

SELF-CHECK

Continued Research

Advances in brain research, neuroscience, and the study of attachment over the last two decades allow us to understand how ACEs and trauma play an immense role in mental and physical health outcomes. Continuing research and advances in science explore how changes in gene expression impact the brain's and organ systems' responses to stress, including the way our DNA is read and transcribed. Trauma can become embedded into cultural norms and

2+ ACEs	Twice the odds of hospitalization due to autoimmune disease
4+ ACEs	2 times more likely to be overweight or obese
	2 times more likely to develop heart disease, cancer, and autoimmune disease
	2.5 times more likely to smoke
	3.5 times more likely to develop chronic obstructive pulmonary disease (COPD)
	5.5 times more likely to have alcohol dependence
	10 times more likely to use intravenous drugs
	32.6 times more likely to have been diagnosed with learning & behavioral problems
6+ ACEs	Life expectancy can have a 20-year difference
7+ ACEs	3 times more likely to develop lung cancer
	3.5 times more likely to have ischemic heart disease; leading cause of death in United States

FIGURE 4.1. ACEs Health Risks (Burke, Hellman, Scott, Weems, & Carrion, 2011; https://www.cdc.gov/violenceprevention/childabuseandneglect/acestudy/; https://www.nhlbi.nih.gov/health-topics/ischemic-heart-disease)

cause increased risk of health issues related to stress-response systems to be passed down from generation to generation, indicating that "intervention with one family generation enhances the protective resources for the next generation, which might prevent intergenerational ACE transmission" (Larkin, Felitti, & Anda, 2014, p. 7). An individual's level of resiliency in coping with childhood adversity can depend "on the genetic background of the individual and his/her exposure to adverse stimuli in prenatal and/or postnatal life (developmental influences)" (Charmandari, Tsigos, & Chrousos, 2005, p. 275). Romero, Robertson, and Warner (2018) explain:

> Generational trauma begins when a population endures a mass trauma, such as colonization or slavery, and the psychological and physiological effects of this trauma manifest within the affected population. The symptoms of this trauma are passed onto the next generation, who will exhibit similar behavioral and health conditions. Recent epigenetics research is starting to uncover a biological basis for this reality. Researchers have found that exposure to trauma and chronic stress can change the expression of certain genes that impact the body's response to stress. As a result, people impacted by trauma, and their offspring, can be genetically predisposed to develop depression, PTSD, type 2 diabetes, and other deleterious conditions. (p. 50)

It is crucial for educators and school staff to play intentional roles among the interrelated systems that heavily influence the experiences of our youth so we can begin to disrupt harmful intergenerational cycles and begin passing down approaches that promote healing. Although signs of toxic stress may manifest in childhood, effects may continue undetected throughout the life span of an individual.

Impact of ACEs on Learning

We learned in Chapter 2 about the different types of stress-response systems and how certain levels of stress impact our ability to learn. Toxic stress develops from children experiencing frequent and prolonged hardships that cause sustained activation of the body's stress-response systems without access to a buffering adult (Center on the Developing Child, 2019). This may not only result in negative physical health outcomes but can also harm cognitive development and the architecture of a child's developing brain. Experiences of childhood maltreatment contribute to the disruption of developmental processes such as attachment and emotional regulation, which often leads to diminished academic performance and mental health (Romano, Babchishin, Marquis, & Frechette, 2015). ACEs have a profound impact on children, especially those who are experiencing toxic doses of stress from adversity without adequate and consistent support from at least one adult in their lives. Neglect and/or abuse during childhood can have serious detrimental effects on academics and behavior that continue into early adolescence and throughout the teen years (Kendall-Tackett & Eckenrode, 1996). A child's health and bodily systems can become so excessively strained from experiencing frequent adverse conditions that the accumulation of toxic stress may not manifest as visible symptoms until well after the triggering event, making it extremely difficult to detect any indication of childhood adversity and trauma. According to Perry (2002):

> Traumatized and non-traumatized children often have very different cognitive experiences in the classroom: The calm child may sit in the same classroom next to the child in an alarm state, both hearing the same lecture by the teacher. Even if they have identical IQs, the child that is calm can focus on the words of the teacher and, using the neocortex, engage in abstract cognition. The child in an alarm state will be less efficient at processing and storing the verbal information the teacher is providing. (p. 200)

How would you know if your classroom was a safe environment for students? Describe what you think a classroom would look like if it was not an emotionally safe environment and the teacher expected everyone to take risks in class (answer questions, contribute to discussion, etc.) while penalizing their grades as a consequence of not participating?

SELF-CHECK

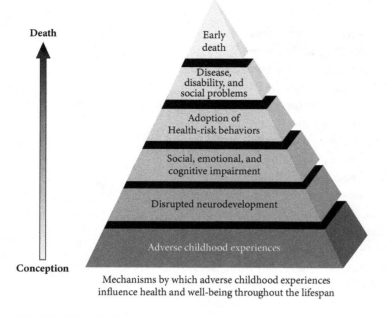

Death

Conception

Early death

Disease, disability, and social problems

Adoption of Health-risk behaviors

Social, emotional, and cognitive impairment

Disrupted neurodevelopment

Adverse childhood experiences

Mechanisms by which adverse childhood experiences
influence health and well-being throughout the lifespan

FIGURE 4.2. ACE Pyramid

We can see from Figure 4.2 how critical it is to understand the impacts of ACEs and trauma on learning. Classrooms and school climates that prioritize physical and emotional safety to buffer effects of traumatic stress can contribute to healing processes for students and school employees. Students struggling with ACEs may also significantly benefit from an environment that provides multiple opportunities for learning self-regulation to support pathways toward successful learning. A difficult challenge in schools is the potential for ACEs to exist in learners and not be acknowledged by school staff or lead to a mislabeling of behavior partly because "the time delay between exposure during childhood and recognition of health problems in adult medical practice is lengthy" (Felitti et al., 1998, pp. 255–256), which includes mental health. You can see from Figure 4.2 that in the amount of time between initially experiencing ACEs and the adoption of health risk behaviors toward the top, it is likely that students may go years without anyone recognizing what is going on in their developmental systems. Without recognition of trauma's negative effects on a child's developing systems, a child may unfairly be assigned punitive consequences for neural, cognitive, social, and emotional impairments that are out of their control yet are expected to have been mastered in the eyes of adults. As mentioned before about mirror neurons in Chapter 2, Romero, Robertson, and Warner (2018) remind us that "If your school or school district is assessing and assigning students living with adverse childhood experiences to special education classes, your school or school policies are actually retraumatizing them" (p. 72).

Although ACEs may exist for many students, they are commonly unrecognized by school personnel who have not had opportunities for training or professional development related to ACEs. This becomes challenging for educators and school staff, since assumptions may easily be made about students that could negatively influence the ways that adults approach them, possibly fostering a climate of disconnection and mistrust. Despite well-intentioned efforts to help struggling students succeed academically, adults in schools may seek concrete explanations for behaviors as a means of coping with their own frustrations and stress about not having the skills to help such students. The students may "have a hard time identifying what emotions they are feeling and finding ways to communicate them in a healthy manner. Emotional self-regulation skills must be taught, modeled, and reinforced for these students, and it may take a considerable amount of time and effort to learn and integrate. This process of emotional maturation is further hindered when our ACEs students live in active trauma" (Romero, Robertson, & Warner, 2018, p. 68). Some students with trauma from ACEs may struggle with focusing, memory, executive functioning, understanding cause and effect, or processing information (Cole et al., 2005). These challenges may present as barriers to academic success and can lead students to cope with the stressors and shame of academic struggle through other behaviors related to issues with deflecting blame, taking responsibility, maintaining healthy connections, and other skills that fellow peers may have already developed.

It can become very difficult for adults in schools who are not equipped with knowledge about trauma and ACEs to maintain their composure and not take student behaviors personally when attempting to provide support or hold such students accountable. It is during these critical moments that adults hold the power to decide whether we want to disrupt possible negative patterns (offering ourselves as buffering adults) or contribute to them. The way we approach these types of situations relies heavily on our own wellness and capabilities for self-regulation.

Some students struggling with experiences of trauma may still be able to achieve exceptionally high levels of academic success that are associated with displays of extreme anxiety or perfectionist mindsets (Robertson & Warner, 2018; Romero, 2019). A common misconception about students in this situation is that their level of functioning is not a concern, since their grades have not been affected. This may lead us to overlook or dismiss their possible internal struggles with unrealistic expectations, harsh self-criticism, challenges with overcoming obstacles, facing tasks requiring novelty, coping with rigorous pressures, and other concerning behaviors that could signify high levels of toxic stress that remain undetected. A buffering adult can help to soothe such high levels of anxiety and stress by observing and becoming emotionally responsive to students' needs. Students are more inclined to develop increased trust in an adult when they notice the adult is taking time to prioritize students' emotional needs over academic content, making efforts to connect during these moments of possible distress. As adults in the schools, if we can maintain our own patience and calm states to be able to use a trauma lens in these types of situations, we can be better prepared to notice signs when a student shows struggles with extreme sensitivity to making mistakes, receiving basic feedback,

Reflection

If a secondary-level student makes a mistake, either during classroom learning or in social situations, what tone do you use with them when correcting or addressing it? What language or words do you use? What do you think your facial expressions and body language communicate to them? If a professor or supervisor/manager used the same tone, gestures, facial expressions, etc. when speaking with you about a mistake you made, would you feel encouraged or discouraged?

overcoming what may be generally accepted as a minimal setback, avoiding challenges and failure, and many other possible behaviors that may indicate a history of unresolved trauma. Without training and awareness of ACEs, we miss out on opportunities to provide support and healing environments for these students who may be enduring toxic stress from experiences such as extreme punishments or blaming at home or deeply conflicted feelings about family/cultural expectations to uphold a false image of perfection to the outside world. We will learn about behaviors associated with trauma histories in more detail in the next chapter, titled "Recognizing Trauma Responses."

In some cases, decisions about what we consider are in the best interests of students in the learning environment can exclude the social emotional and relational aspects of learning necessary for developing successful life skills that have lasting impacts on students' futures, especially with regard to employment, higher education, family, and relationships. Isolating the social emotional learning component and identifying it as a separate topic from academic subjects can result in unintended consequences, such as a school culture where subject-specific teachers become accustomed to dismissing the idea of incorporating relational skills into their repertoire of abilities as educators. Some of the benefits of integrating social emotional learning with academic content will be discussed further in Chapter 7.

Some of our approaches to students may unknowingly be triggers for one or more prior trauma-inducing experiences. The way students experience our interactions with them helps determine how they will respond to us. Some of these disagreeable behaviors may actually be rooted in either a conscious or unconscious experience that automatically signals danger to the brain, triggering the body to act in the best way it can to avoid physical or emotional harm at that very moment. Students with a trauma history "are bound to experience current stressors with an emotional intensity that belongs to the past, and that has little value on the present" (Streeck-Fischer & van der Kolk, 2000, p. 911). As adults, we can easily fall into the trap of aiming our focus and energy toward taking a student's responses personally. Our defensiveness may be fueled by a triggering of our own assumptions when we feel threatened by the possibility that our competence as educators and support staff may be in question. Sometimes we are too overwhelmed ourselves to recognize that we are in a prime position to disrupt reinforcing patterns of negativity that may be fueling high levels of toxic stress for students. Romero, Robertson, and Warner (2018) encourage educators by helping us to see that

> once we understand that trauma and ACEs impact the neurological and physiological functioning of ACEs students, we can begin to have insight and compassion. Their outbursts or meltdowns are no longer simply acts of defiance. Instead they are reflexive, and often ingrained, attempts made by the child to feel safe. Unfortunately, these attempts to feel safe can appear as efforts to control their internal or external environment by shutting down or acting out, neither of which are going to help the child succeed in school or make it easy for us to teach them. Therefore, we are tasked with the responsibility of finding ways to help the ACEs child downregulate their stress response so that they can learn. (p. 70)

Taking a pause to intentionally utilize a trauma-informed lens can help school staff members strengthen their own skills of recognizing signs of potential trauma and ACEs. Immediate action can be taken by intentionally becoming a buffering adult and consulting with an appropriate professional in the building or on campus, such as an administrator, school counselor, or other designated staff member equipped to support and utilize information toward generating plans for a team approach.

Challenging Belief Systems

One great challenge in moving toward a trauma-invested lens is developing an open mind about recognizing that every single one of us is vulnerable to toxic stress and traumatic experiences, regardless of where we grew up or where we come from. Existing research indicates increased risks and negative consequences associated with child abuse for children living in poverty compared to children with higher socioeconomic status and access to more resources (Johnson-Reid, Drake, & Kohl, 2009). The ACE Study provides valuable data that helps challenge existing biases about students and family populations from various backgrounds that may be negatively charged.

An example of a bias can be associated with an "us vs. them" mindset in regard to public and private K–12 schools or public schools in affluent communities compared to schools located in impoverished areas. A strong assumption from one side could be that *they don't have the problems we do*, so the *other* could not possibly understand what *our* students are experiencing. Do the biological processes of the stress-response systems differ among students from different backgrounds, such as private versus public schools or West vs. East Coast?

Souers and Hall (2019) discuss the detrimental effects that holding assumptions about students and families with limited information can have on our efforts to provide safety and support to students in need. This becomes counterproductive to the essential work we claim we are intending to address and improve. For example, some common assumptions about students attending private schools include labeling them as *rich*, *spoiled*, and *entitled*. Assumptions can help drive attitudes that dismiss possible struggles these students may be facing, leading to a learned culture in which family pressures to uphold society's expectations about them become channeled through anxiety, isolation, and stigma attached to seeking help. The troubling assumption that *affluent families are immune to trauma* can contribute to the stigma associated with the real issues some students may be struggling with, such as alcohol and substance use and/or domestic violence in the home, parental separation or divorce, suicidal ideation related to bullying or perfectionism, absent parents, or emotional neglect, among other various adverse experiences. These very same issues also have the capacity to affect students from other SES backgrounds attending public schools. From Chapter 3, we know that a child's worldview and learned behaviors are shaped by patterns of previous interactions and experiences. Students from seemingly wealthy families may have adapted to beliefs driven by their particular cultures or communities, which include messages implying they are not allowed to seek support due to various risks. Asking for help can portray weakness in some cultures and may result in social disdain, jeopardizing the reputation and status of the family.

In discussing secrecy associated with upper-income groups, Burke Harris (2018) mentions that the risk of having reputations of false perfection is high, and the continued secrecy is what actually perpetuates the cycle. The combination of ACEs, family or cultural denial, and insufficient support can negatively disrupt a child's developmental processes (Larkin & Records, 2007). The pressure to maintain a certain image may leave students feeling they have no other option than to deal with their stress in isolation. The lack of safety and unmet emotional needs some students experience may exacerbate unhealthy stress levels and lead to risky behaviors as coping mechanisms to alleviate unbearable suffering.

Assumptions may also arise about students from lower SES regarding behavioral and/or academic expectations. Stressful challenges such as poverty, violence in communities, and abuse affect many families and students in several ways. It has been shown that children experiencing poverty have much higher levels of chronic stress than children in more affluent communities (Almeida, Neupert, Banks, & Serido, 2005). Diminished emotional and cognitive functioning can result from dealing with the toxic stresses of higher exposure to abuse and violence and overburdened caregivers trying to meet basic family needs. Jensen explains that students "raised in poverty need more than just content; they need capacity" (2009, p. 54). Our roles as supportive adults in the schools are a key piece of the resiliency puzzle, as "systemic risks such as poverty and oppression may be compounded, or moderated, by interpersonal relationships" (Larkin, Felitti, & Anda, 2014, p. 5). Students experiencing trauma can be provided opportunities to flourish in a school setting that emphasizes a priority on healing relationships with buffering adults to combat the harmful effects of ACEs. For students who transfer from private to public educational settings or vice versa, assumptions about where they came from can create difficulties with transitioning into a new school environment. These assumptions can play a big part in how new students are treated, not only by their new peers but also by the school staff.

Though it may be true that different school settings may offer distinct experiences based on several factors such as the surrounding communities, school culture, accessibility of resources, SES of student population, etc., each student's unique experiences and responses

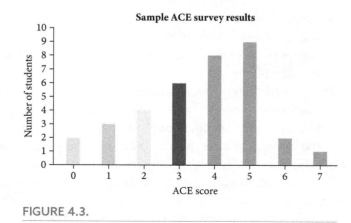

FIGURE 4.3.

must also be considered. High levels of toxic stress and experiences of childhood trauma for different individuals have a commonality in the negative influences on the development of a growing child's neural and biological systems. Developing a trauma lens can lead the way toward understanding that "Trauma-informed approaches and strategies help to foster compassionate, inclusive, and resilient classrooms in which all students, especially those impacted by ACEs, develop skills for academic success and healthy behavior" (Romero, Robertson, & Warner, 2018, p. 70).

Practice #1

Anonymously collect ACE scores from the class (for example, you can use slips of paper placed in a jar or online tools such as SurveyMonkey) and format the data visually using a chart, graph, etc. An example is provided in Figure 4.3. Adjustments such as dividing into smaller groups may be made to accommodate class size.

1. Discuss your thoughts about the group's data on the graph. Compare it to other groups (if applicable).
2. What were your assumptions about the prevalence of childhood trauma before reading this chapter? Did you have previous knowledge/learning opportunities about ACEs and trauma before this class?
3. Imagine that everyone in your group is 10 years old and the data remained the same. How could this information be helpful for your teachers and school staff in supporting your learning and development?
4. What could you consider as reasons for possible inaccuracies or bias in any sample of adult ACE scores (over age 18)?

CASE EXAMPLE

Emily is a sixth grader in middle school. A few of Emily's teachers notice she frequently comes to class with a tired disposition. The teachers occasionally overhear Emily mention to classmates in passing that she did not get much sleep the night before. A few teachers have begun complaining to each other about how Emily is "not doing anything" and that they are frustrated, often asking, "Why can't she just get her work done? It's not that hard." As the school year progresses, Emily increasingly struggles with academics in addition to having frequent social conflicts that often result in Emily's hostile reactions toward friends and peers. One of Emily's teachers consults about academic and behavior concerns with the school counselor. The school counselor meets with Emily the next day during lunch to discover that Emily's parents have been in the process of a high-conflict divorce for the last six months and that Emily stays up nights helping with her older sister's crying infant, since she feels bad that her sister always seems sad and moody. The counselor notices during their meeting that Emily displays mildly shaky hands and seems to be extremely hypervigilant about her surroundings, as she is easily distracted and turns her focus toward any random sound that is heard from outside the counselor's office. Emily lives with her sister, niece, biological father, and his girlfriend; however, her father and his girlfriend are rarely home. When they *are* physically at home, Emily experiences constant blame from everyone in the home for not helping enough and for being a "spoiled brat" and "useless" when she says she needs to study or do some homework.

DISCUSSION QUESTIONS

1. What is Emily's ACE score, based on what you have read? What are your thoughts about Emily's potential ACE score as she transitions into high school?

2. At the first signs of "not getting work done," what proactive steps could the teachers have taken to support Emily to prevent her from falling as far behind as she did?

3. Considering what you have learned so far about trauma and ACEs, what would you say to your colleagues if they were sitting with you during lunch discussing Emily's academic performance as described in the case example and none of you were aware of Emily's home life?

4. Following up on Question #3 above, imagine that all of Emily's teachers learned about Emily's experiences at home. One teacher says, "That's no excuse. She could do her homework during lunch. Who knows what she's doing when she's supposed to be listening during class?" Would you respond to these comments? Why or why not? If so, how would you respond?

Chapter Summary

The increasing recognition of the prevalence of ACEs is necessary for informing communities and various professions about the significance of shifting toward trauma-informed practices, including in education and health care. As research on ACEs continues to emerge, other types of childhood trauma are being discovered in addition to the three types identified by the ACE Study. ACEs have the potential to cause toxic levels of stress, which can negatively impact a child's behavior and developmental systems. Without acknowledgement of possible trauma or proper supports in place, the long-term effects of ACEs can have serious health consequences into adulthood. School staff members can contribute to healing processes for students struggling with ACEs by learning about childhood trauma and maintaining consistently calm, patient, and understanding dispositions to foster nurturing relationships. This is possible when the adults in schools prioritize their own self-care and work collaboratively toward using best practices to support student needs.

Connect and Reflect

1. After calculating your own ACE score and learning about the potential risk of developing various health outcomes based on an ACE score, what are your initial thoughts about how you might be affected by ACEs?

2. Did you have buffering adults in childhood you could turn to for safety when you experienced distress?

3. Do you notice a connection between ACEs and health risks within your family or the family of a close friend?

4. Think about the students you currently work with or have worked with in the past. Based on what you know about their experiences and/or home environments, would any of them score points on the ACE survey? Does this change the way you view(ed) students regarding your assumptions about or approaches to them?

5. Do you notice a difference in behaviors or academic performance in students who may have higher ACE scores than others?

6. How would learning about ACEs be beneficial to teachers, administrators, support staff, and parents in a school community?

Extended Learning

Burke Harris, N. (2018). *The deepest well: Healing the long-term effects of childhood adversity*. New York, NY: Houghton Mifflin Harcourt.

Felitti, V. J., Anda, R. F., Nordenberg, D., Williamson, D. F., Spitz, A. M., Edwards, V., ... Marks, J. S. (1998). Relationship of childhood abuse and household dysfunction to many of the leading causes of death in adults: The Adverse Childhood Experiences (ACE) Study. *American Journal of Preventive Medicine, 14*, 245–258. doi:10.1016/S0749-3797(98)00017-8

Forbes, H. T. (2012). *Help for Billy: A beyond consequences approach to helping challenging children in the classroom*. Boulder, CO: Beyond Consequences Institute, LLC.

Hughes, K., Bellis, M. A., Hardcastle, K. A., Sethi, D., Butchart, A., Mikton, C., ... Dunne, M. P. (2017). The effect of multiple adverse childhood experiences on health: A systematic review and meta-analysis. *Lancet Public Health, 2*(8), e356–e366. doi:10.1016/S2468-2667(17)30118-4

Jensen, E. (2009). *Teaching with poverty in mind: What being poor does to kids' brains and what schools can do about it*. Alexandria, VA: ASCD. Retrieved from https://acestoohigh.com

Romero, V. E., Robertson, R., & Warner, A. (2018). *Building resilience in students impacted by adverse childhood experiences: A whole-staff approach*. Thousand Oaks, CA: Corwin.

Credits

Fig. 4.1: Source: https://www.ncbi.nlm.nih.gov/pmc/articles/PMC3119733/.

Fig. 4.2: Source: https://commons.wikimedia.org/wiki/File:The_ACE_Pyramid.gif.

Chapter 5

Recognizing Trauma Responses

W E NOW KNOW from Chapter 2 that the limbic system copes with traumatic experiences through instinctive responses—such as fight, flight, or freeze—to overwhelming threats. When children are continuously exposed to unhealthy surroundings composed of neglect, abuse, loss, violence, violation of trust, etc., their emotional health becomes compromised by modes of survival. This ***survival mode*** temporarily impairs access to higher cognitive functions and activates responses from the limbic system, which can be unhealthily prolonged and exhibited through various behaviors from students. Such behaviors ultimately indicate the effects of traumatic stress on brain functioning and learning.

The harmful effects of not having the capability to consider or recognize potential underlying trauma in a student often result in punishment and consequences for those who violate our values regarding a sense of "right" and "wrong" (Echo, 2018). This often compels adults without trauma education to mislabel students and respond accordingly, such as engaging in well-intentioned lectures for students with goals of teaching about making "good" choices vs. "bad" choices. In some cases, frustrations with continuous behavior(s) may lead to this teachable topic becoming a repeated conversation so often that its overuse results in eventual lack of effectiveness. For example, can students truly reflect on choices they have made when they become dysregulated and their amygdalas hijack their prefrontal cortexes, leaving the higher executive functioning parts of their brains inaccessible? Access to the logical problem-solving functions of the brain adults expect students to use during moments of dysregulated behavior(s) is literally blocked, and the very things that would help a student gain

Learning Objectives

1. What are some common trauma responses from students in the learning environment?
2. How can we recognize particular student behaviors as indicators of trauma?
3. Can some indicators of trauma overlap with other learning difficulties and lead to mislabeling of a student?
4. How can adults strongly influence the climate of the learning environment and impact students' capacity for learning?

access to those higher brain functions—*calm, safety, validation, and unconditional regard*—are the opposite of what we may offer through our verbal and nonverbal responses. When considering learning expectations in the school setting, van der Kolk (2014) explains that

> traumatized people so often keep repeating the same problems and have such trouble learning from experience. We now know that their behaviors are not the result of moral failings or signs of lack of willpower or bad character—they are caused by actual changes in the brain. (p. 3)

School staff that become trauma-informed are aware of the challenges with understanding that behaviors stemming from toxic stress and traumatic experiences have many similarities to other diagnoses that impact learning in the classroom, such as ADHD. Chapter 6 discusses resources and strategies for schools to begin efforts toward becoming trauma-informed and emphasizes the value of providing continuous staff training about relevant topics to ensure that all adults have access to the most current research to enhance our abilities and confidence to support students appropriately. For now, it's sufficient to note that a child with an overloaded amount of neural activation from perceived threats, such as our responses to them, has the potential to have altered brain development in regard to emotional, behavioral, and cognitive functioning (Perry, 2001). Limited executive functions may be a factor of increased sensitivity to minimal stress-inducing situations for a child and could result in misinterpreting a child's responses as impulsive, hostile, oppositional, unmotivated, manipulative, or other types of behaviors without considering the child's efforts to cope with traumatic stress through patterns of responses triggered by reminders of past trauma (Streeck-Fischer & Van der Kolk, 2000).

When students perceive our responses to them as negative due to our own frustrations or impatience, their behavior and attitudes may escalate and set off our own nervous systems, often leading to unnecessary and stressful power struggles for both individuals. Classroom behavior of children struggling with trauma can present as confusing to adults, which may lead to misinterpretation about the motivation behind such behavior and disconnected relationships with peers or adults in the school environment (Cole et al., 2005). If a student's behavior or the relationship does not improve after consistently dealing with situations in this way, why would we think the student's attitude or behavior will change *this* time? What is getting in the way of our willingness to change our style of communication and approaches so children can feel a sense of safety? Perry (2006) elaborates by explaining,

> When children start to misbehave, our initial impulse to punish and deprive them often serves us poorly; we tend to see children who are whiny and demanding and aggressive as "spoiled" and "indulged" rather than recognizing that these qualities usually arise from unmet needs and unexplored potential, not from having too much or feeling too good. In order for a child to become kind, giving, and empathetic, he needs to be treated that way. Punishment can't create or model those qualities. Although we do need to set limits, if we want our children to behave well, we have to treat them well. (p. 243)

Another way of looking at this is to think of using a key to unlock a door. Imagine you are coming home from a long day of work or school and feel exhausted and hungry. Once you arrive at your front door, you insert your key, but it does not turn to unlock the door. Nobody is home to open the door for you, and there is no spare key available or hidden anywhere. You are confused as to why it does not work and repeatedly attempt to reinsert the key, hoping it will open the door. After about the 10th time trying the key, you begin to get very upset and impatient because you are tired and hungry, and there is no logical explanation for your key not working. Although that same key has not been successful the first 10 times since you arrived home, you continue to insert the key and hope that it will work *this* time. If it did not work the first 10 times, is there a high possibility that is will work the 11th time? If you are unwilling to adapt and problem solve to find solutions to attain your goal of getting inside the house (e.g., checking for an unlocked window, calling a locksmith, contacting someone who has a spare key, etc.), you might continue to try the same method of using your key and expect different results.

This is similar to supporting students with potential trauma backgrounds. You may not be aware of all or any of the details regarding their past traumas and may be confused or frustrated with their presenting behaviors at any moment. If your communication style is received negatively by a student struggling with trauma and they react by perceiving your interaction as a threat, you have the capability to continue the reinforcing cycle of negative interactions and exacerbate the negative quality of the relationship. This can become counterproductive to any desire or efforts toward improving rapport with the student and creating a consistently safe learning environment. Your options are either continuing an unsuccessful power struggle that elicits negative feedback patterns between you and the student or shifting your perspective to recognize that your responses to the student may be a source of stress based on their past experiences. Adults often do not realize the adult brain is fully (or almost fully) developed, yet the expectation for students is to have the same level of self-management and cognitive functioning as adults.

Children struggling with trauma may experience states of terror from being triggered. In that moment, they may not be able to process what others say to them, nor might they be able to verbalize what they are feeling or what their needs are. Teachers who struggle with managing difficult behaviors can begin to recognize the need for safety and provide a climate of healing so students are not reexperiencing trauma. Just as persistent threat responses increase the risk for long-term symptoms in a child, factors influencing a calming of threat responses will help reduce the risk of reexperiencing trauma (Perry, 2001). Effectively showing students that we are safe and will accept them unconditionally for who they are requires consistent patience from adults. The most critical yet difficult moments for creating such meaningful experiences are when students attempt to push us away with behaviors that can be extremely hurtful for us. Our own resiliency in supporting students through this process helps to build resiliency in the students themselves. A long-term benefit of adults not giving up on them is their increased potential for healing pathways toward not giving up on themselves.

Once school staff members are aware of the neurobiology of potential trauma and the effects of emotional safety, a priority on relationships can be established through continuous practice. There are some cases when a student exhibits enough resiliency to feel okay enough to continue learning after a potentially triggering event or interaction during the school day. For another student who may be struggling with unresolved trauma, the lack of access to certain basic needs, such as a positive human connection with an adult, may result in dysregulation and a persistently activated amygdala throughout the course of the day. This may easily be translated into the student manifesting behaviors that are misinterpreted as intentionally disrespectful, disruptive, defiant, etc. The all too familiar outcome of consequences may fulfill the immediate goal of sprinting to "get through the curriculum," which creates missed opportunities for human connection that could foster positive social-emotional development for the student. What might be missing for the student experiencing difficulty with self-management or focus is a sense of *consistent connection and attunement from an adult*, the prime ingredient for emotional safety and healing from trauma. Learning to shift our way of being with students can feel threatening to the traditionally accepted approaches many instructors continue to practice. These instructors may wrongly assume that any shift will negate their intentions and efforts. Ironically, both the instructors and the students are doing the best they can with what they have in the moment to survive. The current research on trauma and interpersonal neurobiology is allowing us to reflect on the facts that we can do better and that we have the capabilities to do so if we are willing to invest in enhancing our knowledge base.

A report published by Massachusetts Advocates for Children titled *Helping Traumatized Children Learn* (Cole et al., 2005) emphasizes the significance of schools and teachers in providing a learning environment that fosters a supportive school community that allows students suffering from trauma to achieve academic success. It provides relevant research on the impact of childhood trauma on classroom learning, behavior, and relationships and includes various ways trauma can potentially affect a child's success in school and present as difficulties for educators in the classroom. As discussed in Chapter 2, fight, flight, freeze behaviors are instinctive ways our bodies respond to overwhelming perceived threats as a result of the amygdala's intent to protect us from danger. Since many children's responses to traumatic experiences vary and do not align perfectly with a "fixed" list of symptoms, it is often difficult to link the various academic and behavioral issues they face with a formal diagnosis. Children with a history of ACEs that include exposure to violence may develop symptoms based on numerous factors, such as frequency, type, and intensity of the violence, the resiliency level of the child, and the presence of a safe, secure, and nurturing home environment (Perry, 2001). It is beneficial for school counselors, teachers, administrators, and support staff to be informed about various indicators of trauma as a way to consider it as a potential factor in misbehavior and recognize that positive, supportive approaches are powerful tools for preventing future recurring triggers from contributing to a student's distress and difficulties in the school setting.

Below are some potential indicators of trauma offered in *Helping Traumatized Children Learn* (Cole et al., 2005) as a resource to enhance our knowledge in considering what may be interfering with a student's progress in school so appropriate approaches and modifications may be made toward a more supportive learning environment. It is important to remain aware of the possibility that signs exhibited by students with trauma histories may be overlooked, and not every student with trauma symptoms should be assumed to be struggling with a trauma background. This is not an exhaustive list, as individual responses vary and substantial research on this topic continues to evolve and enhance our increased understanding of the role trauma plays in children's academic, social, and emotional development.

IMPACTS OF TRAUMA ON LEARNING AND BEHAVIOR

- Difficulty processing written and verbal information
- Inhibited ability to use language to communicate and express needs, feelings, and self
- Struggle with maintaining coherent conversations and narratives (energy may be primarily focused on nonverbal cues instead of verbal content)
- Challenges with organizing information sequentially
- Lack of motivation/perseverance in academic tasks, goal setting, and delayed gratification (internalized sense that they have no control over what happens to them)
- Unsuccessful with behavior management methods requiring comprehension of cause and effect
- Struggle to understand perspective of others (jeopardizes skills related to problem solving and drawing inferences from texts)
- Easily distracted or overstimulated; trouble focusing (thoughts dominated by heightened anxiety about safety)
- Dissociation from classroom teaching, activities, or other tasks (increased anxiety about catching up and keeping up with peers)
- Difficulty with emotional self-regulation
- Inability to plan, hope, or anticipate (lack of optimism and expectation of failure)
- Weak impulse control
- Difficulty reading emotional cues
- Distrust of others
- Verbal or physical aggression toward self/others
- Oversensitivity/distorted perceptions of others' actions toward them
- Disinterested or disconnected from surrounding environment (avoids painful or uncomfortable feelings)
- Defiant behavior or freezing (not responsive to expectations of class or teacher)
- Withdrawn behavior
- Perfectionist qualities (fear of disappointing others, easily distressed, gives up on challenging tasks)

> ### Reflection
>
> After reviewing the above list, have you noticed some of these behaviors in any of your students? If so, did you assume something was "wrong" with them, or did you pause to wonder if something else might be impacting their behavior?

Because inconsistency in academic or social behaviors is common and some children may also develop depression, anxiety, or self-destructive tendencies, helping students master social and academic skills is vital to the healing process. For more information about this report, please refer to the section under "Extended Learning" at the end of this chapter. A free link to this book is also available in PDF form.

Additionally, SAMHSA funded a project published by The National Child Traumatic Stress Network (NCTSN) titled *Child Trauma Toolkit for Educators* (2008). This included a list of behaviors conveniently categorized by specific school level that may help in recognizing potential signs of trauma in students and is organized in the chart below.

PRESCHOOL	ELEMENTARY	MIDDLE SCHOOL	HIGH SCHOOL
• Separation anxiety or clinginess towards teachers or primary caregivers • Regression in previously mastered stages of development (e.g., baby talk, bedwetting/toileting accidents) • Lack of developmental progress (e.g., not progressing at same level as peers) • Re-creating the traumatic event (e.g., repeatedly talking about, "playing" out, or drawing the event) • Difficulty at naptime or bedtime (e.g., avoiding sleep, waking up, or nightmares)	• Anxiety, fear, and worry about safety of self and others (clingier with teacher or parent) • Worry about recurring violence • Increased distress (unusually whiny, irritable, moody) • Changes in behavior (increase in activity level, decreased attention and/or concentration, withdrawal from others/activities, angry outbursts and/or aggression, absenteeism) • Distrust of others, affecting children interactions • A change in ability to interpret and respond appropriately to social cues	• Anxiety, fear, and worry about safety of self and others • Worry about recurrence or consequences of violence • Changes in behavior (decreased attention and/or concentration, increase in activity level, change in academic performance, irritability with friends/teachers/events, angry outbursts and/or aggression, withdrawal from others or activities, absenteeism • Increased somatic complaints (e.g., headaches, stomachaches, chest pains)	• Anxiety, fear, and worry about safety of self and others • Worry about recurrence or consequences of violence • Changes in behavior (withdrawal from others or activities, irritability with friends/teachers/events, angry outbursts and/or aggression, change in academic performance, decreased attention and/or concentration, increase in activity level, absenteeism, increase in impulsivity, risk-taking behavior) • Discomfort with feelings (such as troubling thoughts of revenge) • Increased risk for substance abuse

(Continued)

FIGURE 5.1. Recognizing Trauma (National Child Traumatic Stress Network, 2008)

(Continued)

PRESCHOOL	ELEMENTARY	MIDDLE SCHOOL	HIGH SCHOOL
• Increased somatic complaints (e.g., headaches, stomachaches, over-reacting to minor bumps and bruises) • Changes in behavior (e.g., appetite, unexplained absences, withdrawal angry outbursts, decreased attention) • Over- or under-reacting to physical contact, bright lighting, sudden movements, or loud sounds (e.g., bells, slamming doors, or sirens) • Increased distress (unusually whiny, irritable, moody) • Anxiety, fear, and worry about safety of self and others • Worry about recurrence of the traumatic event • New fears (e.g., fear of the dark, animals, or monsters) • Statements and questions about death and dying	• Increased somatic complaints (e.g., headaches, stomachaches, overreaction to minor bumps and bruises) • Changes in school performance • Recreating the event (e.g., repeatedly talking about, "playing" out, or drawing the event) • Over- or under-reacting to bells, physical contact, doors slamming, sirens, lighting, sudden movements • Statements/questions about death and dying • Difficulty with authority, redirection, or criticism • Re-experiencing the trauma (e.g., nightmares or disturbing memories during the day) • Hyperarousal (e.g., sleep disturbance, tendency to be easily startled) • Avoidance behaviors (e.g., resisting going to places that remind of event) • Emotional numbing (e.g., seeming to have no feeling about the event)	• Discomfort with feelings (such as troubling thoughts of revenge) • Repeated discussion of event and focus on specific details of what happened • Over- or under-reacting to bells, physical contact, doors slamming, sirens, lighting, sudden movements • Re-experiencing the trauma (e.g., nightmares or disturbing memories during the day) • Hyperarousal (e.g., sleep disturbance, tendency to be easily startled) • Avoidance behaviors (e.g., resisting going to places that remind them of the event) • Emotional numbing (e.g., seeming to have no feeling about the event)	• Discussion of events and reviewing of details • Negative impact on issues of trust and perceptions of others • Over- or under-reacting to bells, physical contact, doors slamming, sirens, lighting, sudden movements • Repetitive thoughts and comments about death or dying (including suicidal thoughts, writing, art, or notebook covers about violent or morbid topics, internet searches) • Heightened difficulty with authority, redirection, or criticism • Re-experiencing the trauma (e.g., nightmares or disturbing memories during the day) • Hyperarousal (e.g., sleep disturbance, tendency to be easily startled) • Avoidance behaviors (e.g., resisting going to places that remind them of the event) • Emotional numbing (e.g., seeming to have no feeling about the event)

Outside the classroom, Echo (2017a, 2018) describes additional behaviors that help us recognize potential trauma in others:

- Panic, anger, hypervigilance
- Paranoia
- All-or-nothing perspective (black-and-white thinking)
- Sensitivity to light and sound
- Fear of open or crowded spaces

- Reenactment (tendency to perceive everything as a betrayal to validate one's own beliefs)
- Physical disconnection from body
- Loss of intimacy
- Shame

Stigmatizing Behavior

Do we need to know the details of a child's trauma history in order to help them in the moment during an overwhelming experience that they may perceive as a "crisis"? Rather than seek out these details when students struggle to cope with unmanageable levels of distress or fear, it is helpful and less stressful for adults to offer a climate of safety, give students what they need emotionally, and recognize particular behaviors as a cry for help because appropriate ways of doing so have not yet been modeled or learned. Although having background information about a student's trauma history helps to positively shift an adult's perspective in supporting the student through behavior struggles, this will not always be the case. We must do our best to be emotionally prepared to support students who lack their own awareness of how their puzzling behavior or misbehavior may be an indication of significant stress from overwhelming experiences because "these students are expected to learn while managing an internal storm of fear and pain. As educators, we frequently experience the brunt of our students' emotional pain often without full knowledge of its cause. … [W]ithout proper supports in place, teaching students impacted by trauma can feel like walking in a minefield uncertain of which move is going to trigger an explosion" (Romero, Robertson, & Warner, 2018, pp. 68–69).

If we can understand the detrimental effects of imposing unreasonable consequences and punishments on students for acting out their pain in the only way they have learned to do so, we can then acknowledge that our unrealistic expectations for them—to describe or verbalize their feelings and make better behavioral choices—may be adding more anxiety to their existing overwhelming stress levels generated by trauma. In practicing a state of curiosity and open mind about what a student might be communicating through their behavior(s), we can relieve some of their stress through the way we interact and begin to experience the long-term positive effects of having the student feel cared for and understood by us. Creating emotional safety and meaningful relational experiences can turn tense situations into opportunities for healing potential trauma. Shifting away from a judgmental perspective also helps to lessen our own defensiveness and the all-too-familiar stress of feeling that student behaviors are personal to us.

In some cases, an adult in the school may not be aware that their own style of interactions or approaches with a particular student may be triggering a potential memory of a past traumatic experience that holds a strong relational context for the student. When we experience disconnected relationships with students who regularly feel judged and dismissed by our style of interactions with them, a pattern of exclusion and stigma against the students is potentially created. It may be difficult to accept that students may be only responding to their perceptions of how they experience us, which is one of the most challenging barriers to understanding that adults have a powerful influence on how the cycle of interactions can begin. In addition to learning about the neurobiology of trauma, our ability to develop a trauma-informed lens requires reflections into ourselves that includes making intentional efforts to maintain a high level of compassion for others and self, patience, self- awareness, and wellness (self-care will be discussed in Chapter 7).

For educators and support staff who have adapted to a mindset of immediately viewing students in a negative light once behaviors arise, this may be the only coping style these adults have learned to adopt during overwhelming moments based on their own unique experiences. Especially if an adult did not get their own needs met at a particular time during earlier life experiences and is having to deal with student behaviors, it would only make sense that the adult might hold an unwavering opinion of "I had the same troubles or worse when I was young, and I got through it just fine," or "Back in my day, we just got through things." For some adults who struggle with awareness of their own traumas, it may be challenging to practice compassion and empathy for students struggling with behaviors manifesting from traumatic experiences.

Figure 5.2 demonstrates how the climate of a classroom or other areas of a school where students interact with adults (cafeteria, gym, hallway, library, office, etc.) can be greatly influenced by the energy and attitude the adult(s) offer to the learning environment. When asked to reflect about what they enjoy and do not enjoy about school or learning, students across multiple grade levels often report they do not enjoy learning when a teacher seems to be in a bad mood, inflexible with expectations, or disinterested in listening and caring about what the students have to say. What matters to students is not what the adults assume they are offering to students but what the adults are *communicating* to the students through their behavior, as described in the top area of Figure 5.2. Notice that the classroom or school environment established in the top area is filtered into two possible student perspectives based on how they receive the adult's interactions and nonverbal communication. The perspective to the left is composed of mindsets and perceptions of students who may be struggling with experiences of stress or trauma. If a triggered amygdala causes a student to exclusively focus all of their energy on monitoring the teacher's temperament in class, processing new information would be difficult for that student. The perspective to the right is an example of how a nontraumatized student can apply all of their energy to learning and processing new information, since the presence of any substantial

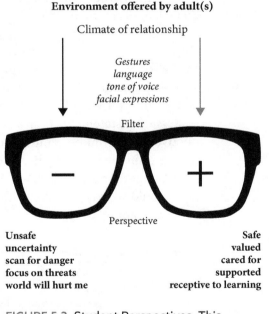

Environment offered by adult(s)

Climate of relationship

*Gestures
language
tone of voice
facial expressions*

Filter

Perspective

Unsafe	Safe
uncertainty	valued
scan for danger	cared for
focus on threats	supported
world will hurt me	receptive to learning

FIGURE 5.2. Student Perspectives. This demonstrates how students may experience people, events, or environments through a negative or positive lens.

threat does not require their attention throughout the class period or school day. For this student, the classroom experience is positive, and the brain is calm enough to engage in new learning. Keep in mind that the actual event is not different for each lens. The difference lies in the experience of the student(s).

With the overwhelming amount of responsibilities placed on adults working in schools, a common way that school personnel relieve high levels of stress is to vent frustrations to a colleague through belittling, mockery, and/or sarcasm about particular students. Although it may feel good and may help relieve stress in the moment due to the sense of bonding, the mirror neurons firing between two such adults are actually creating stronger neural pathways of thinking that could lead down a spiral of negativity where the pattern of conversations entail putting people down and complaining about anything and everything in the workplace. This rabbit hole can easily become counterproductive to any efforts of maintaining staff wellness and positive energy in a school, which is necessary for a workplace that intends to become a trauma-informed community.

Intentionally choosing to model a discussion about concerns and issues in a professional and courteous manner helps us refrain from making strong assumptions about things when we may not know the details of a student's story. This supports a trauma-informed perspective, as it shifts to a more respectful view of the student and takes into consideration the student's unique experiences that may be contributing to their challenging behavior. To stay in a supportive frame of mind, a professional perspective with colleagues can help steer the conversation toward solutions instead of venting and feeling miserable about the assumption that changes are impossible.

Practice #1

In the following exercise, imagine you are having a conversation with a colleague in a school setting and they share with you the statements from the left column below. Think about how you would reframe the comments/thoughts from the left column into more professional statements that would help generate a discussion encouraging a more productive way of brainstorming ideas for solutions while maintaining respect and dignity for the individuals being discussed. The first two provide examples of what a more professional and productive statement might look like; however, there is no "fixed" answer. How would you reframe the first two statements to align with your personality and style of communication?

Assumptions/Judgments	Reframe
He's getting on my nerves. He won't stop talking in class, interrupts all the time, and constantly gets up out of his seat. I keep telling him to stop. He blatantly does not listen to me to make me mad.	He keeps talking, interrupting, and getting out of his seat in class and I keep reminding him to stop. He can't seem to stop, so I'm not sure what I can do at this point because I feel like I've tried everything I can. Do you have any ideas I can try?

Assumptions/Judgments	Reframe
I think she purposely does things so she can get attention from everybody. She acts like she doesn't know what to do in front of everyone, but I give directions at least twice to the class. I know she knows what to do.	*Something might be going on with her that we don't know about. It seems that she tries to get everyone's attention, but not in appropriate or positive ways. I don't know how to support her.*
He keeps distracting the class and making everyone laugh on purpose. I'm sick of dealing with him, and he needs to get it together because I won't tolerate such disrespectfulness.	
She's a lost cause. All she does is stare out the window, and she never turns anything in.	
He's constantly defiant. He talks back and is rude all the time. I can't deal with it anymore, so I just ignore him. He needs to be medicated.	
She's a complete nightmare to deal with. She always blames other people and doesn't take responsibility for her own actions. Then she cries whenever you try to talk about what she did to contribute to the situation.	
Mr. Smith is the worst teacher. His class is always out of control, and he lets them get away with anything.	
Ms. Smith's kids only like her because she bribes them with rewards and treats. That's the only way she can get students to like her.	
Nothing really happens when we send students to the counselor. They don't get in trouble or have consequences, and all they do is talk or play. The counselor's too nice and too soft to help.	

Our Own Trauma Histories

It may be challenging for some adults to consistently and objectively provide a safe harbor for all students if they have not been able to get past their own "stuff." In other words, some adults may have not taken the time to reflect and make sense of how earlier experiences have influenced their own current states of being, which can greatly enrich relationships with others in all relational aspects of an individual's life, such as work, school, social circle, family, etc. Children struggling with trauma experiences during which their basic needs were not met may not be aware of their own feelings, and this lack of awareness can carry into adulthood along with impaired development of certain relational skills.

Children and adults with chronic trauma related to abuse and neglect are potentially burdened with the challenge of developing secure interpersonal relationships, which can become difficult during stressful states and could trigger such dehumanizing experiences that might be transferred onto others (Streeck-Fischer & van der Kolk, 2000). From a neurobiological standpoint, *we are not capable of accessing the parts of the brain that allow us to express empathy and compassion for others if we ourselves are experiencing high or toxic levels of stress or anxiety*. For example, consider why airline passengers are reminded during the in-flight safety instructions or video to fasten their own oxygen masks before helping others during an emergency. In order to take care of other individuals, we need to make sure we take care of ourselves first. It would be difficult for adults in schools to give the highest quality of care to students if their own wellness is not intact.

When an adult has past experiences of trauma that have not been acknowledged, resolved, or made sense of regarding their influence on the adult's own development, it can become a barrier to understanding one's self, becoming fully present with others, being open to connection with others, demonstrating flexibility and kindness, and many other qualities necessary for maintaining healthy relationships. The simple practice of presence as we experience a broad range of feelings without allowing emotions to take over allows us to strengthen our levels of resiliency, and at times, our expectations of students can become a hindrance to our ability to stay present (Siegel, 2013).

Practice #2

Echo (2018) developed a list of guided reflection questions to help practice maintaining a trauma-informed lens when we find ourselves dealing with stressful and challenging moments with students and colleagues. If adults have the awareness to emotionally self-regulate, they are better equipped to recognize an individual's trauma or sense another's needs. The following questions also focus mostly on *you* instead of the other person in any given situation.

1. Without judgment, what was my reaction (physical, emotional, mental), and how did I then respond?
2. Did the behavior offend my personal values?
3. Did it offend my learned social values?
4. Was it triggering my trauma?
5. Was I witnessing a trauma response in the other person?
6. Am I able to find compassion for myself and the other person?
7. Did I respond by punishing, shaming, shunning, or badgering?

Think about a past situation when you were extremely frustrated by another individual's behavior and you developed harsh judgments or may have not reacted as your best self. Describe the context of what happened from your perspective and then answer the reflection questions above.

Calming Ourselves to Calm Others

When we become extremely frustrated or upset with students, it is sometimes difficult to notice the positive behaviors of students because we are not able to get our own minds and bodies into a calm state in order to access the parts of our brains responsible for logic and rational thinking. One of the consequences of personally strengthening our own negative neural networks about a particular student is that it can create a strong influence on tarnishing our ability to intentionally create shared experiences of positive connection where both the student's and teacher's neurons fire together in sync to construct new positively connected neural pathways. It can also cause teachers themselves to enter negative frames of mind, as the negative experiences with one student begin to distract from all the other positive interactions during the course of a day.

This process takes patience and authenticity from educators as they become responsible for initiating safe and caring experiences. Shifting attitudes and perspectives about how we interpret student behaviors takes much practice and may feel just as challenging and uncomfortable as attempting to change personal habits.

In particular, it is extremely important that even if a student with a potential trauma history did not receive high marks but you sense they did the best they could under the circumstances, the student is acknowledged for their efforts to attempt or engage in the work. One of the most healing aspects of reversing the effects of trauma for students is communicating to them that they are worthy of you taking moments to notice them while helping them feel that you will not give up on them despite any behaviors that attempt to frustrate or push you away.

For us as adults working in the school setting, our attitude and energy are significant factors contributing to the type of learning environment offered to students. For those students entering the classroom struggling with trauma experiences, this means focusing all our efforts and time only on preparing learning materials, lessons, schedules, etc. is not adequate for being able to meet the basic needs essential to a child's healing toward feeling emotionally safe enough to learn.

There are times when an adult may deliberately use positive words to speak to a child, yet the adult's tone, body language, and facial expressions create a contradicting experience for the child receiving the words. Adults in schools and parents/caretakers are often unaware that they are highly influential models for emotions and behaviors (both positive and negative) that children learn to imitate through carefully observing expressions, emotions, and actions. Because our attitudes and energy set the tone for our work environment in schools, the practice of self-checking throughout the day to monitor our own states of mind can effectively model valuable qualities contributing to safety and increased student learning. An experience that is potentially traumatic may result in the child mirroring either the calm and supportive presence or the dysregulated behavior of a teacher, parent, or other caregiving adult (Streeck-Fischer & van der Kolk, 2000).

What may be observed as inattention in the classroom could be due to a student's energy and focus being dedicated to deciphering the teacher's disposition. Or a student who does not demonstrate understanding of concepts being taught in class may not be able to process new information if they **disassociate** from the environment as a coping mechanism for dealing with trauma. It is beneficial for school personnel to be cautious about being drawn into continuous cycles of disconnection with students, since such energy impairs their abilities to take in new information.

Practice #3

What is a student's underlying behavior trying to communicate to us? There may be times when we know the details of students' histories and other times when we have absolutely no idea what they carry with them as they enter school. One of the key ways to support students the best we can is to use our trauma lens to consider how dysregulated emotional behaviors may be a student's way of communicating their experiences and reaching out for help. Below are examples of student behaviors an adult may observe in the classroom or general school environment.

The goal of this exercise is to practice consultation about students using a trauma-informed lens to foster a supportive mindset that contributes to personal wellness and professionalism in the workplace. Discuss with a partner or group whether you think the student's behavior in each brief scenario below suggests a trauma background, even without having any knowledge of the student's history. For any scenarios you feel may be an indication of trauma, use your knowledge from Chapter 2 to discuss whether the student is demonstrating fight, flight, freeze, dissociation, or a combination of responses. Next, if you have time, consider how you might respond, or share ways in which you've seen teachers respond to similar situations.

1. A student in the classroom constantly gets up from their seat and wanders off to random areas of the room. When the teacher prompts the student to get back on task, the student does not return to their seat right away.
2. Two students in the same class often criticize each other and do not get along. One of the students takes the other's backpack when nobody notices and throws it in the dumpster outside.
3. A student always asks for seconds immediately when the class is given any type of edible treat or there is a party/celebration in the classroom with food.
4. A student repeatedly interrupts the teacher during lecture and points out how the information being presented is incorrect.
5. A student takes three or four times longer than their peers to finish an assignment that includes creating artwork.
6. On the playground, a student interrupts a game and steals the ball. That student then throws the ball at another group of students, hitting one student in the face.
7. A student is often caught stealing school supplies out of their peers' desks.
8. A student often corrects their peers whenever they get something wrong or make a mistake.
9. When a student is called on in the classroom to answer a question, the student often stares at the teacher without facial expression and does not respond.
10. A student claims that everyone is purposely against them, even when peers try to include that student in activities or peers try to apologize after conflicts.
11. A student consistently cries and blames others whenever there is a peer conflict that is in the process of being resolved.

12. The class is watching a video. During a sad moment, some students get teary-eyed. One student says out loud, "Why are you crying?"

13. A student typically does not eat lunch. When an adult asks them about not eating, the student repeatedly replies, "I'm not hungry."

14. A student seems to put minimal effort into classwork and turns in assignments quickly so they have opportunities for free time.

15. A student rarely responds or makes eye contact with you when you talk directly to them, even when you say hello.

16. You notice a student roll their eyes or make a comment under their breath whenever you address them in front of the class.

CASE EXAMPLE #1

Mr. Scott is a kindergarten teacher and is gathering his students after a 20-minute recess period outside on the school playground. As soon as his students line up in a single-file manner, Mr. Scott positively comments on how impressed he is with how fast the class follows his instructions and begins to walk the line back to the classroom. Once Mr. Scott reaches the classroom door, he holds it open for the students to enter and announces that they will be having snacks next. Mr. Scott asks all students to use the bathroom if they wish but that everyone must wash their hands and scrub with soap before they can eat a snack.

Mr. Scott notices that one of his students, Nathaniel, does not approach the bathroom line or either of the two lines for the sinks. Mr. Scott walks over to Nathaniel to calmly ask if he needs to use the bathroom, and Nathaniel shakes his head "no." Mr. Scott then asks Nathaniel to wash his hands and explains that the dirt from recess will get into his food if his hands are not washed. Nathaniel shakes his head again in the same manner. Mr. Scott further explains to Nathaniel that he will not be able to have a snack until his hands are washed. He tries to help by gently nudging Nathaniel toward the sinks. Nathaniel's behavior becomes dysregulated as he refuses and begins screaming and crying. Since Mr. Scott is the only adult in the room at the moment and the rest of the class has almost finished washing their hands, Mr. Scott says to Nathaniel, "Why don't you take a break over here while I help the other students get settled with a snack?" Mr. Scott swiftly proceeds to engage in his normal class routine for snack time by walking around to check if students retrieved snacks from their backpacks. He hands out boxes of raisins to students who don't have any snacks.

Reflection

Pause for a moment before you continue reading. How would you handle this situation if you were Mr. Scott?

Ms. Gomez, the school counselor, walks by Mr. Scott's classroom and hears Nathaniel crying. She knocks, pokes her head in the classroom, and sees Nathaniel crying near the inside of the door.

Ms. Gomez enters the classroom and smiles at Mr. Scott as he walks over to explain in a whisper, "He's upset because I explained that he needs to use soap and scrub his hands before snacks. His hands are very dirty. He's getting some space to calm down." Ms. Gomez walks over to Nathaniel with a warm smile and calmly asks, "You don't want to wash your hands?" Nathaniel shakes his head "no." Ms. Gomez reaches her hands out with palms facing up and asks in a caring tone, "Would it be okay if I looked at your hands?" Nathaniel offers his hands to Ms. Gomez, and she notices how red and cold they are from the weather outside. Ms. Gomez asks Nathaniel, "Does it hurt when you wash your hands?" Nathaniel nods his head and stops crying as he continues to frown. Ms. Gomez then asks, "Can you show me where it hurts on your hands?" Nathaniel points to the knuckle area on one hand. "Can I help you wash them gently with soap so that it doesn't hurt?" Nathaniel nods "yes" and voluntarily walks over to the sink with Ms. Gomez to wash his hands. Ms. Gomez first checks to make sure the water is warm, since Nathaniel's hands are red and feel cold. Mr. Scott grabs some paper towels for Nathaniel and says to him, "I can gently help you dry your hands so it doesn't hurt." At this point, Nathaniel is calm and allows Mr. Scott to help dry his hands. Mr. Scott throws the paper towels in the trash can and gestures to take Nathaniel's hand. Nathan immediately reaches out to hold Mr. Scott's hand as they walk together to get Nathaniel's snack from his backpack.

DISCUSSION QUESTIONS

1.   Were any of Mr. Scott's or Ms. Gomez's actions inappropriate in response to Nathaniel's behavior? If so, which ones, and why do you think so?
2.   Were any of Mr. Scott's or Ms. Gomez's actions helpful in calming Nathaniel? Which ones, and why do you think so?
3.   What kind of responses from Mr. Scott do you think would have negative outcomes?
4.   Why do you think Ms. Gomez immediately left the classroom right after the situation instead of staying in the classroom to talk about it with Mr. Scott?
5.   Did the situation ultimately result in changed behavior? Did the situation ultimately provide factual information for future use?

CASE EXAMPLE #2

On a Monday morning, one of the school buses arrives at Blue Mountain Middle School. As the students exit the bus and enter the school building, they are greeted by the assistant principal, Mrs. Fallon. Jeremiah, a seventh grader in the crowd of students walking in from the bus, walks past Mrs. Fallon with an emotionless facial expression and his hood on as she says aloud, "Good morning, Jeremiah. Take your hood off in the building." Jeremiah does not respond or take his hood off and continues to walk into the building and down the hallway. Mrs. Fallon turns around toward Jeremiah and follows him while yelling out loud in a commanding tone, "Jeremiah, I said good morning. You need to greet me back and take your hood down." Mrs. Fallon catches up to Jeremiah, reaches for his hood from behind and yanks it off his head. Jeremiah continues to walk away without turning back to look at Mrs. Fallon. Mrs. Fallon then states in the same commanding tone, "You're lucky I'm in a good mood today. The next time I say good morning, I expect you to show respect and say good morning back." Jeremiah immediately puts his hood back on.

One of Jeremiah's teachers, Ms. Rowling, observed the entire incident from her doorway. Ms. Rowling does not have a close relationship with Jeremiah; however, she has never really had any problems with Jeremiah's behavior in her class. Ms. Rowling continues to stand at her door and watches Jeremiah stop to use his locker from the corner of her eye. Jeremiah closes his locker and begins to walk in the direction of Ms. Rowling's classroom. As Jeremiah walks near Ms. Rowling's door, Ms. Rowling makes eye contact with him and offers a soft, warm smile. She quietly says, "You don't seem like you're okay." Jeremiah stops at Ms. Rowling's door to talk.

Jeremiah:	*I haven't slept all weekend.*
Ms. Rowling:	*Is everything okay at home?*
Jeremiah:	*My dad left.*
Ms. Rowling:	*What do you mean "left"?*
Jeremiah:	*He's just gone. All his stuff is gone. Since Friday.*
Ms. Rowling:	*Do you know where he is? Has he contacted you?*
Jeremiah:	*No.*
Ms. Rowling:	*Who's taking care of you at home?*
Jeremiah:	*It's supposed to be my mom, but she's always working. She's never really home.*
Ms. Rowling:	*Are you okay if we walk together to the counselor's office to let her know that you probably are not in a good mode for learning and being in class? There is a couch in one of the empty offices nearby if you'd like to rest for a little while. I'm sure she wouldn't mind.*
Jeremiah:	*Okay.*
Ms. Rowling:	*Let me help you with your hood. Is that okay?*

Jeremiah nods, and Ms. Rowling gently reaches out both hands to take his hood down. They walk together to the counselor's office.

DISCUSSION QUESTIONS

1. What are your thoughts about how Mrs. Fallon interacted with Jeremiah?
2. If Ms. Rowling had not stopped Jeremiah to talk, he may have gone through the whole school day without any adult knowing about what had happened over the weekend. How might that have impacted Jeremiah's academics? Would you expect him to complete all of his work for the week on time if you were Ms. Rowling?
3. Why do you think Jeremiah allowed Ms. Rowling to take his hood down?
4. Is there anything you would do afterwards to follow up and/or support Jeremiah?

Chapter Summary

Signs of toxic stress can manifest as early as childhood and may impact the learning process for students in different ways. As educators and adults in the school environment, we are responsible for paying attention to student behavior and taking action professionally to support the needs of students, especially when that behavior may seem puzzling or seems to require our extra attention. To increase success with our responses to students and keep our own stress levels in check, it is vital for adults in schools to have the knowledge, training, patience, and self-care to recognize symptoms of toxic stress when they are presented in front of us. If we become more aware of how students' overactive stress response may be inhibiting their executive functioning, it would be much easier as adults to understand that the root of a student's behavior is not about us personally, leaving our own systems of regulation to be primed and ready to provide the best care we can offer to students.

Being trauma-informed does not automatically mean we know exactly how trauma appears in students, nor does it guarantee that previous trauma training will be utilized in situations requiring our care. Our ability to recognize student behavior that communicates a need for support or connection helps to separate the behavior from feeling like it is a personal attack on us as adults in the learning environment. The more purposeful reflection time we spend on understanding ourselves and our responses to others, the more opportunities we allow ourselves to practice using a trauma-informed lens with our students and colleagues. Adults in schools who develop increased skill sets in recognizing potential trauma behaviors can respond to urgent student needs by providing a safe climate and establishing trust through an authentic relationship, even without initially knowing students' personal histories.

Connect and Reflect

1. In reference to Practice #3, what are some other behaviors you have either observed or may remember exhibiting yourself in a classroom that adults might find puzzling?

2. Are there certain behaviors or habits you find irritating in others or that you have absolutely no patience for? Describe what those might be and what they might be communicating.

3. What might personally be getting in the way of you having enough patience and understanding to tend to a student's needs if they are exhibiting difficult or disruptive behaviors that would activate your amygdala?

Extended Learning

Cole, S. F., O'Brien, J. G., Gadd, M. G., Ristuccia, J., Wallace, D. L., & Gregory, M. (2005). *Helping traumatized children learn: Supportive school environments for children traumatized by family violence.* Boston, MA: Massachusetts Advocates for Children.

Siegel, D. J., & Hartzell, M. (2014). *Parenting from the inside out: How a deeper self-understanding can help you raise children who thrive* (10th anniversary ed.). New York, NY: Jeremy P. Tarcher/Penguin.

Sours, K., & Hall, P. (2019). *Relationship, responsibility, and regulation: Trauma-invested practices for fostering resilient learners.* Alexandria, VA: ASCD.

Credits

Chapter 6

Healing Through Safety

B UILDING SAFE, AUTHENTIC, and connected relationships with every single member of the school community is at the heart of trauma-informed school cultures. A student's sense of physical and emotional safety is based on whether the adults in the environment are knowledgeable and aware about ensuring that current interventions for behaviors refrain from triggering potential retraumatization for students. Staff collaboration and modeling of strong relationships among colleagues contributes to a healthy school climate and sends the message of safety and security to students.

Physical and Emotional Safety

The brain prioritizes emotions, since they are associated with how children experience the people and places in their lives. Reflecting back on Chapter 3, Maslow's hierarchy of needs indicates safety and security as primary needs, which include physical and emotional safety, toward the base of the triangle. As Olson (2014) explains the neurobiology of safety, he emphasizes the significance of reflecting on the difference between *being* and *feeling* safe. An entire school's culture must be consistently intentional in ensuring students *feel* safe through unconditional positive relationships built on mutual trust and acceptance, which can be modeled for students by adults in the school. This process originates from the relationships among teachers and administrators and filters down to the students. Teachers can only perform at their best in this way when they themselves feel supported and trusted by the school's leadership, as they also have a need to feel emotionally and physically

Learning Objectives

1. What characteristics of a classroom offer safety to all students?
2. What is emotional safety?
3. How can discipline practices potentially cause a student to experience retraumatization in a school?
4. What are some consequences of school staff members neglecting self-care?
5. What are the five core competencies for CASEL?
6. What are some examples of how students and adults can benefit from social-emotional learning and mindfulness?

safe in order to model a sense of calm and set the tone for optimal learning.

For individuals learning about emotional safety as a fairly new concept, it may be easier to recognize and understand the concept of physical safety over emotional safety, since you can usually rely on physical evidence of harm. This can be challenging for many individuals who do not feel emotionally safe because, since you cannot actually see the hurt, it is more difficult to prove your case to others who might immediately develop assumptions that "you're okay" when you may not actually be. Because threats to emotional safety are associated with interpersonal relationships, they can affect us in many different areas of our lives, such as school, work, family, friends, and social interaction. Social media, texting, and other forms of electronic communication add another complex layer to interpersonal relationships, potentially causing higher levels of anxiety for students' developing brains.

Students who associate school with a feeling of safety develop skills and enough confidence to take risks in the learning environment. This enables students to feel emotionally safe enough to express ideas, ask questions, collaborate, and attempt novel experiences without fear of consequences for making mistakes. Consistent feelings of safety in schools help maintain calm amygdalas in students and strengthen neural pathways that allow new information to be readily access by the higher-level thinking brain. According to Anderson et al. (2001), the verbs represented in Bloom's taxonomy from Figure 6.1 describe the hierarchal classification of cognitive processes by which thinking individuals encounter and work with knowledge. Since trauma can negatively affect a child's cognitive development and brain architecture, it is helpful for school personnel to become aware of the significance of general sequencing related to basic needs and learning in the classroom. Based on what you have learned about brain processes impacted by trauma, access to the lowest-order verbs may not necessarily be achievable for a dysregulated child without first providing basic physiological needs and a sense of safety associated with Maslow's hierarchy of needs (see Figure 3.1 in Chapter 3).

Since there is no *one-size-fits-all* solution to finding successful ways for children to feel safe, the process of learning what the child's needs are can last longer than we expect. Getting to know who students are and building trusting relationships with them can allow us to understand what triggers them and what we need to do to become buffering adults in the schools. For example, expressing feelings may help one student get regulated, but it may feel unsafe for another triggered student. Perry (2006) explains that "Because safety is critical to recovery and force creates fear, coercive therapies are dangerous and ineffective for victims of trauma" (p. 246). In the context of

---

Reflection

Describe any current or past people, places, things, or experiences that help you feel a sense of safety. What aspects or qualities of these experiences helped you feel safe? How would you "create a safe space" where a student would be able to feel understood and heard? What would that look like?

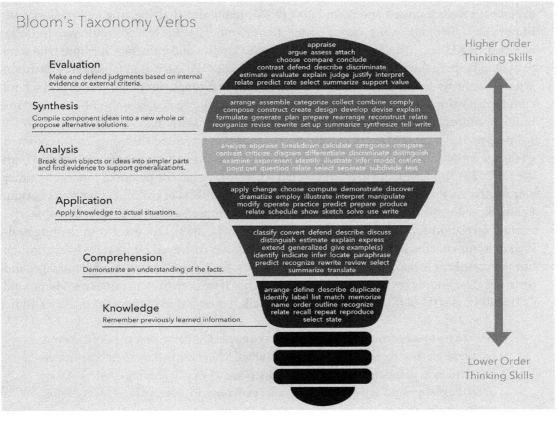

Bloom's Taxonomy Verbs

Higher Order Thinking Skills

Evaluation
Make and defend judgments based on internal evidence or external criteria.

appraise argue assess attach choose compare conclude contrast defend describe discriminate estimate evaluate explain judge justify interpret relate predict rate select summarize support value

Synthesis
Compile component ideas into a new whole or propose alternative solutions.

arrange assemble categorize collect combine comply compose construct create design develop devise explain formulate generate plan prepare rearrange reconstruct relate reorganize revise rewrite set up summarize synthesize tell write

Analysis
Break down objects or ideas into simpler parts and find evidence to support generalizations.

analyze appraise breakdown calculate categorize compare contrast criticize diagram differentiate discriminate distinguish examine experiment identify illustrate infer model outline point out question relate select separate subdivide test

Application
Apply knowledge to actual situations.

apply change choose compute demonstrate discover dramatize employ illustrate interpret manipulate modify operate practice predict prepare produce relate schedule show sketch solve use write

Comprehension
Demonstrate an understanding of the facts.

classify convert defend describe discuss distinguish estimate explain express extend generalized give example(s) identify indicate infer locate paraphrase predict recognize rewrite review select summarize translate

Knowledge
Remember previously learned information.

arrange define describe duplicate identify label list match memorize name order outline recognize relate recall repeat reproduce select state

Lower Order Thinking Skills

FIGURE 6.1. Bloom's Taxonomy

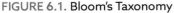

school-wide interventions aimed at de-escalating student behaviors, paying attention to this kind of information can help us become more effective in supporting students in the learning environment and decrease the time gaps between feelings of terror and safety. Effective strategies for helping a triggered child return to a sense of safety include offering a relational connection rooted in genuine care and respect and engaging in mindfulness activities that bring the child into the present moment.

Relationships

One of the most valuable things we can offer to students is modeling healthy and positive relationships, which, "characterized by attachment and belonging, are a critical element for well-being" (Evans & Vaandering, 2016, p. 61). For those students struggling with trauma, school staff members cannot control what happens in their lives outside of our school. What adults in schools can control is a steady intention in ensuring every single student is treated with dignity and respect every moment they are in our care at school. This consistency in providing a predictable environment for students may be the only way they are able to experience feeling valued and seen. Perry (2006) maintains that "healing and recovery are impossible ... without lasting, caring connections to others. What healed children ... the folks who respected them, who were tolerant of their weaknesses and vulnerabilities and who were patient in helping them slowly build new skills" (p. 232). We learned in Chapter 2 how brain science confirms that offering students a sense of safety through our relationships and school climate can calm the amygdala, or *downstairs* brain, so they can access the PFC, or *upstairs* brain, to successfully engage in learning and higher-order thinking.

Interpersonal trauma happens in the context of attachment and relationships, and a common challenge for any individual suffering from such trauma is nurturing a safe relationship (van der Kolk, 2015). The quality of interpersonal relationships has the potential to serve as either a protective factor or as a means for health risks or the effects of childhood trauma (Larkin, Felitti, & Anda, 2013). The antidote for childhood trauma and toxic stress is safe, stable, and nurturing relationships and environments (Burke Harris, 2019). Our priority in creating healing environments for students struggling with trauma is conveyed by what we offer through human connection, such as our voice, tone, words, facial expressions, body language, and proximity. Patience is key, as we cannot have patience if we are not calm ourselves. Hammond (2015) discusses the significance of even the smallest moments of connection with a child:

> You can try to speed the trust-building process, but feeling connected grows slowly and requires time for people to get to know each other. It happens in those small day-to-day interactions as a student comes into the classroom, when you pass him in the hallway or on the playground. It happens in the quiet exchanges we have with a student during an activity or with our subtle body language, whether it's a head nod, a quick smile from across a room, or a gentle hand on a student's shoulder when he is struggling with completing his work. Students will begin to feel cared for when they recognize and experience familiar forms of affection and nurturing. (p. 77)

At home, many students may lack appropriate models of healthy ways to interact with peers and adults. These students, whether or not they are dealing with trauma, need our help with learning how to develop and maintain nourishing interpersonal relationships. Students with trauma histories may experience an uphill battle in trying to forge connections with peers and adults because their manifested behaviors from trauma can isolate them from peers and school staff due to fear or frustration. We can begin to develop a trauma lens by understanding that power struggles between students and school staff can be seen as students' attempts to feel safe by gaining control of their environment in a world where they feel mostly powerless (Craig, 1992). For example, if we trigger a student struggling with a trauma history by expecting them to automatically comply with a last-minute schedule change without any explanation or consideration for their potential feelings of fear or insecurity, we are setting ourselves up to become a walking danger zone for that student's brain. This may be avoided by having already established a trusting relationship with the student beforehand and becoming a buffering adult in the moment by calmly supporting their needs.

Link Box

Access a brief video titled *Every Opportunity* from the Atlanta Speech School from the link below, and then answer the reflection questions:

https://www.youtube.com/watch?v=VxyxywShewl

REFLECTION QUESTIONS

1. What are your initial reactions to watching the difference between a supportive and unsupportive school environment?
2. Have you encountered negative or positive experiences of adults in your childhood similar to those of this student? How did that affect your sense of safety around those adults?
3. Are there times when you may not be aware that students perceive you as exhibiting similar negative responses as the adults in the first half of the video?
4. Do you think the quality of relationships presented in the video can impact student learning, whether or not a student has a trauma history?

A benefit of a trauma-informed culture is that the collective buy-in from a majority of the staff results in healthier connections among the adults in the school as they work toward supporting each other in addition to helping students. When you have access to supportive (not negative) emotional connection with a fellow colleague whenever you are feeling overwhelmed, the repeated calming effect of this process helps you practice regulation and minimize prolonged periods of stress. Another benefit of fostering healthy relationships among staff is improved and consistent communication to help prevent any possibility of an adult–student relationship being used against a struggling student to cause emotional harm.

For example, a teacher might be frustrated with a student struggling with trauma because they are not meeting academic or behavioral expectations in the classroom. Even though the teacher is aware that the student regularly checks in with the school counselor, since the teacher has not yet been trained about the impacts of trauma on learning, they assume the student is trying to avoid work by going to the counselor's office. After the teacher unsuccessfully attempts to use all the behavioral management techniques they know, the teacher starts placing conditions on the student that require completed classwork before granting permission to see the school counselor. Not only does the student's behavior not improve, the student now has conditional and limited access to the one buffering adult in the school who can offer a space of safety and security in order to calm the student's stress-response system and help return to manageable functioning. Perry (2006) describes how this type of intervention is one where adults "take a punitive approach and hope to lure children into good behavior by restoring love and safety only if the children start acting 'better'" (p. 244).

Fostering Resiliency and Wellness

According to Wolpow, Johnson, Hertel, and Kincaid (2016), resiliency is the ability of an individual or community to withstand and rebound from stress and can be fostered by offering unconditional positive regard in a safe and caring environment. Student resiliency is a necessity for any school environment that wishes for all students to flourish academically, emotionally, and socially.

Teachers and school staff sometimes have tendencies to expect students' resiliency levels to be adequate for school, whether it involves academic work or social interactions. There is a difference in resiliency levels between students with secure attachments and those struggling with childhood trauma. It is so important for adults in schools to consider how some student behaviors that frustrate us and may lead us to label as "lazy," for example, can very well be rooted in earlier experiences beyond the student's control. Adults who communicate their frustrations to that child, whether verbally or nonverbally, only add to the shame such behavior is rooted in. Van der Kolk explains (2014):

> Securely attached children learn what makes them feel good; they discover what makes them (and others) feel bad, and they acquire a sense of agency: that their actions can change how they feel and how others respond. Securely attached kids learn the difference between situations they can control and situations where they need help. They learn that they can play an active role when faced with difficult situations. In contrast, children with histories of abuse and neglect learn that their terror, pleading, and crying do not register with their caregiver. Nothing they can do or say stops the beating or brings attention and help. In effect they're being conditioned to give up when they face challenges later in life. (p. 113)

Students are often told what not to do by adults without being given models for the adults' expectations, and then reprimanded for not getting it right. This *guessing game* for students can create enough stress to inhibit production of their best work if the adults in these situations are not supportive and attuned to the students, ultimately leading to mistrust of the adults and school system. Many adults have valuable power in modeling what they want to see in their students. The effectiveness of this relies on whether students sense consistency and genuine respect among the staff. For example, imagine a student who is repeatedly reprimanded by a teacher for talking with peers during class lectures. One day, a guest speaker presents to that same class and the student notices that the teacher is socializing with a colleague in the back of the room while the guest is presenting to the class. What messages might the student receive from these observations?

In order for adults in schools to develop the capacity for successfully guiding a triggered child toward safety, their own wellness must be maintained. Adults who intentionally manage stress in their personal lives will be better equipped to acknowledge their own trauma histories and reflect on what activates stress for them. If we are not careful, our own lack of self-care can unconsciously spill into our work with students. Abel, Eggleston, Green, and Poe (2018) explain:

> Self-aware educators **R**ecognize how their behavior can affect students. They dedicate conscious planning to avoid detrimental reactions when faced with vulnerable decision points to foster a safe and predictable learning environment. Teachers who model neutralizing routines in their classrooms **R**ecognize the importance of resilience of both educators and students. (pp. 85–86)

Self-Care

Since teaching and working with students are highly demanding relational professions, it can become challenging to maintain wellness as adults. **Self-care** is our personal tool kit of strategies for preventing or mitigating symptoms of toxic stress and requires us to pay attention to and nurture our physical, emotional, and mental health needs (Romero, Robertson, & Warner, 2018). It is vital to balance adequate self-care with our obligation to care for students and colleagues, as our ability to effectively support others can be jeopardized (Norcross & Barnett, 2008). Self-care is an ethical mandate for many helping professions, as it helps to serve as a protective factor against the dangers of toxic stress and vicarious trauma.

Romero, Robertson, and Warner (2018) explain the differences between burnout and compassion fatigue from a mental health perspective. In the workplace, **burnout** is characterized as physical and emotional exhaustion as a result of prolonged stress, which can lead to lack of motivation at work. Employees experiencing burnout are likely to have physical and emotional breakdowns. The ongoing stressful experiences of school staff employees can lead to compassion fatigue. **Compassion fatigue** is described as exhaustion, emotional distress, or indifference as a result of demanding workplace obligations to care for others (Wolpow, Johnson, Hertel, & Kincaid, 2016). Romero, Robertson, and Warner (2018) explain:

> Emotional states affect teaching. When professional development does not prepare educators or they don't feel supported with handling the occupational complexities of their role, negative emotions produce hormones that make them sad, angry, fearful, and perhaps forgetful of the ideals that drew them to the profession. They are prone to compassion fatigue and on their way to burnout and making poor decisions about self-care. (p. 64)

Wolpow et al. (2016) describe the negative impacts on educators, as they can easily find themselves engaging and overidentifying with a student who is struggling with trauma. When vicarious trauma is experienced, the adult's effectiveness in supporting that student becomes compromised by impaired professional decision-making and may lead to behaviors such as avoidance of their own feelings to minimize students' experiences, isolation from colleagues, resistance to change, wishing a student would stay home, and numerous requests to remove the student from class (Romero, Robertson, & Warner, 2018).

The prevalence of trauma in schools and the highly demanding nature of school environments can increase the susceptibility of school staff members to burnout, compassion fatigue, and vicarious trauma. Awareness of maintaining appropriate boundaries while supporting students is necessary for the staff member's wellness, and recognizing the significance of this balance helps keep adults focused on their professional roles in the situation.

There are infinite strategies that individuals can incorporate into self-care plans, and it is important to discover what works best specifically for you. Taking care of ourselves and increasing awareness of our own limitations require intentional practice and sometimes a shift in attitude toward understanding that building resiliency in students starts with us. Being deliberate, flexible, and open-minded about trying new activities helps "build and stimulate brain cells, open up channels of creativity, and build up your resiliency capacity" (Romer, Robertson, & Warner, 2018, p. 23). Educators can benefit from engaging in activities that foster connection with others, especially in settings where reflective processing occurs within a relationship. Here are some examples of commonly recommended strategies for self-care (Burke Harris, 2018; Christofferson, 2018; Romero, Robertson, & Warner, 2018):

- Staying hydrated
- Adequate rest and sleep
- Healthy nutrition
- Daily movement and exercise (yoga, dance, running, etc.)
- Grooming and hygiene
- Spending time with family and pets
- Social connection and bonding
- Hobbies such as sports, music, or art
- Mindfulness and meditation (reflection time)
- Relaxation (hot bath, massage, etc.)
- Spending time in nature (walking, hiking, etc.)

The increasing recognition of trauma and ACEs encourages schools to provide professional development about recognizing mental health issues in students, yet staff members may also benefit from learning their own wellness depends on emotional maturity and acknowledgement of their vulnerabilities to stress (Romero, Robertson, & Warner, 2018). School cultures that recognize the value of the capacity to pause, pay attention to triggers, and reflect before reacting can prioritize practices—such as mindfulness, meditation, yoga and, other restorative approaches—that support the mental well-being of teachers and students.

Practice #1

The ProQol (Professional Quality of Life) quiz was developed by Beth Stamm and is widely used in helping professions in which employees assist others who have experienced trauma. It is a tool for assessing an individual's level of vicarious trauma, burnout, and resilience in the workplace. The use of this quiz is for educational purposes only and is not meant to be used for diagnostic purposes or medical advice. The scaled scores may vary for educators based on the time of the school year, as certain times of the academic year typically produce more stress for school staff. Access the website at https://proqol.org or the following link to take the ProQol Self-Score quiz, and carefully follow the directions for self-scoring: https://proqol.org/uploads/ProQOL_5_English_Self-Score.pdf.

Mindfulness

Mindfulness has become increasingly popular in schools for students as well as school employees, as the amount of educational resources available for implementing mindfulness practices continues to rise. Developing our own mindfulness routines can help enrich the school community through presence and modeling valuable skills such as attention, flexibility, intention, and awareness so school staff members may acquire "the attentional and emotional resources and regulatory control they require to create and maintain emotionally supportive classroom climates in which all students can learn" (Roeser et al., 2012).

Siegel (2015) describes **mindful awareness** as an approach to "training the mind that helps us develop the ability to be present with what is happening in the moment and to let go of judgments" (p. 113), which includes meditation as a way of practicing focused attention to support healthier functioning in the body, mind, and relationships. Mindfulness is known to boost resilience, as it is a practice and a way of being that requires cultivation as it deepens over time (Williams & Penman, 2011). "Attentiveness, engagement, competence, and achievement are only possible when a learner's brain is in a receptive state, allowing for calm and mindful response. Mindful activities help train the prefrontal cortex to pay attention, absorb details, and think clearly" (Hawn Foundation, 2011, p. 77). Just as it takes time and practice to develop skills in some-thing you have never tried before, mindful awareness activities require much patience and willingness to practice in order to experience the potential benefits related to mental and physical health. Trauma awareness training in schools includes education on brain science that supports academic success through a focus on social-emotional intelligence.

For individuals of any age, activated stress responses can cause overstimulation of one's biology that may lead to unfavorably reactive behaviors, such as those described in Chapter 5 (Burke Harris, 2018). Without having the space to be able to slow down and take time to collect ourselves, it can be too difficult to manage more arousal than our bodies can handle in the moment. There are many benefits to having resources that help us stay constantly connected with family and friends, yet numerous external distractions exist that lure our focus away from focusing on ourselves, such as smartphones, iPads, television, radio, the Internet, social media, and the convenience of having immediate access to information at your fingertips (Siegel, 2015). A consequence of adapting to such a lifestyle in which this is how the majority of an individual's time is spent may be the lost opportunities for exercising the parts of the brain necessary for present, face-to-face connection and personal reflection. Intentionally tuning in to what is going on in ourselves in a world full of stressors and distraction can help improve our awareness about what may be contributing to some of the ways we respond to other people and situations.

It is necessary for all school staff members to maintain awareness and sensitivity to the fact that some students struggling with more severe cases of trauma may not yet be ready to engage in mindful awareness activities such as yoga and meditation, as it may trigger states of fear that are too triggering for the body to handle. Students may also experience sensory elements in the environment—such as a particular bell or chime or closing of the eyes in dim lighting—that trigger stressful responses. In these cases, such students can be referred to the school counselor or other school-based mental health professional so their needs can be assessed and proper referrals made, if necessary. This is one of the reasons why trauma-informed training includes *all* school employees, as any uninformed adults in a school community are prone to antiquated patterns of making harmful assumptions and judgments about students.

Mindfulness embodies the "practice of being aware of internal thoughts and feelings in a sustained way" (Burke Harris, 2018, p. 107), which can be used as a calming technique for students *and* adults through various exercises such as breathing and movement exercises. According to Nhat Hanh (2009), "Awareness of the breath is the essence of mindfulness. ... The insight we gain from mindfulness meditation can liberate us from fear, anxiety, and anger, allowing us to be truly happy" (p. x). Learning to intentionally regulate our own breathing and heart rate can help soothe our stress-response systems and support emotional equilibrium (Hawn Foundation, 2011). Other aspects of mindfulness that benefit individuals struggling with trauma include the focus on self-compassion and gratitude, as they involve the practice of observation without criticism. In the documentary *Cracked Up* (Esrick, 2018), van der Kolk explains:

> Trauma is usually about a victim trying to make amends. … The most important thing is forgiveness of yourself for having been this vulnerable, as scared, as angry, as frozen as you were. And forgiving yourself for all the ways you have tried to survive. So just take care of that. Just learn to forgive yourself. … That's a big job.

Meditation practice that focuses on self-compassion and kindness may lead to increased positive emotions and reduced physical symptoms of illness (Fredrickson et al., 2008). Optimistic thinking in turn combats rigidity and contributes to flexibility, adaptability, resiliency, and many other skills related to social-emotional learning. You will have an opportunity to research several different resources related to mindfulness and social-emotional learning in the next chapter so that you may become familiar with the types of programs schools may offer to students.

Link Box

Access the link below to view the 1-minute video from David Wolfe of the Holistic Foundation, Inc. (2017): https://jmcrecovery.com/this-school-ditched-detention-for-meditation-and-it-has-worked-wonders/

REFLECTION QUESTIONS

1. If some of your students were displaying skepticism about this program being implemented at your school this year, would you be willing to participate in the activities with the students to promote your support and increase student buy-in?
2. What do you think might be some barriers to implementing this program in a school? How would you try to minimize such barriers?

Practice #2

Research simple breathing exercises that help introduce breath awareness. Choose a brief one to practice that you feel comfortable introducing to a group and that lasts no more than 1 or 2 minutes. In a group, take turns teaching each other your chosen breathing techniques and discuss which one(s) you would be willing to practice as a self-care tool during moments of anxiety or stress and why it suits you.

Social-Emotional Learning

Social-emotional learning (SEL) is the process of teaching skills to promote understanding of how to "manage emotions, set and achieve positive goals, feel and show empathy for others, establish and maintain positive relationships, and make responsible decisions" (Collaborative for Academic, Social, and Emotional Learning, 2019). Benefits of SEL include increased academic achievement and improvements in behavior and attitudes about self and others (Durlak et al., 2011). The Collaborative for Academic, Social, and Emotional Learning (CASEL) is one example of the many resources available for schools to consider when implementing social-emotional programs. It is the most widely used framework for teaching SEL and incorporates five core competencies that may be flexibly taught and used across many settings.

CASEL Core Competencies

1. Self-awareness
2. Self-management
3. Social awareness
4. Relationship skills
5. Decision-making

Practice #3

Research CASEL's five areas of competency by accessing their website at https://casel.org. Write thorough descriptions about each competency to familiarize yourself with the specific skills relating to each domain.

An example of how the third core competency, social awareness, can be applied flexibly in a classroom is to introduce the concept of perspective taking into your classroom practices. Increased empathy and compassion for others and ourselves help cultivate relationships and develop skills in perspective taking. Perspective taking involves intentionally viewing situations from the perspective of someone else, and it requires reflection to help strengthen our understanding of other individuals' behaviors. Students can benefit from multiple activities that consistently require viewpoints through different lenses while encouraging respectful discussions in an emotionally safe environment. Incorporating perspective taking into lessons and activities assists students in learning how to consider different viewpoints and practice impulse control to manage their own anxieties and other reactions in response to different opinions. It also models acceptance and understanding of different beliefs without insults or negatively charged criticism, fostering a low level of stress and allowing the PFC to exercise its higher-level cognitive capabilities. The teacher's presence and modeling of mindful awareness consistently for students throughout the school day can set the tone for whether these meaningful conversations are successful.

Some resources offer programs that integrate SEL and mindfulness, which can be advantageous by focusing on teaching skills and building student capacity for relationship-building skills. Additionally, "children need free time to run and play and learn how to socialize with each other" (Perry, 2006, p. 238). Engaging in physical challenges, the arts, and mindful practices that enhance learning and reduce stress activates both emotional response and executive function networks simultaneously (The Hawn Foundation, 2011, p. 93). Perry (2006) also adds:

> too many young children are spending more and more of their lives in environments so structured and regimented that there is little time to build friendships and get the practice and repetition needed to support empathic caring. Worse yet, time spent with their parents is often limited as well, and what remains is rapidly filled up with hours of homework or, alternatively, hours of television, computers, and video games. Brain development is use-dependent: you use it or you lose it. If we don't give children time to learn how to be with others, to connect, to deal with conflict and negotiate complex social hierarchies, those areas of their brains will be under-developed. (p. 239)

Reflection

Sit in a quiet area and make a list of as many experiences as you can remember when you received gratitude or kind intention from another person or group of people. What were your emotional states during these experiences? What are you doing now in your practice that might help your students feel positively as a result of what you offer in gratitude and kindness?

CASE EXAMPLE

Sienna is a new ninth-grade student in high school who transferred from another district. In the last 2 years at her previous school, Sienna suffered from trauma related to extremely toxic peer relationships and witnessed continuous bullying of a friend on social media. She felt the school staff did not care because they did nothing to address the issue despite several attempts to report different incidents. Sienna is extremely worried and nervous because she does not know any students at the new school and struggles with trusting peers and adults. Sienna currently meets weekly with a private counselor to work on improving confidence, learning how to be assertive, and practicing strategies for how to manage her anxiety when she feels overwhelmed in a social setting. On the first day of school, Sienna walks into her first class a few minutes late because she had difficulty finding the classroom, since it is a much bigger campus than her last school. Sienna takes one of the two open seats toward the front of the class as the teacher gives her a stern glance for being late. The teacher begins the class by discussing expectations and rules, including emphasis on respecting the teacher. Additionally, the teacher states that students do not need to ask permission to go to the bathroom as long as they go one at a time. In the course of that single class period, Sienna experiences the teacher using several demeaning comments accompanied by negative sarcastic tones, such as the following:

Student: *"Where can I find the reading that is due next week?"*
Teacher: *"I already told the class. I'm not going to hold your hand."*

Student:	*"I already learned how to do this a different way from my mom."*
Teacher:	*"Good for you. You have to do it my way if you want credit in my class."*
Student:	*"Is there any extra lined paper?"*
Teacher:	*"Yes. It's on the back shelf where the sign says LINED PAPER (raised voice)"*
Student:	*"I didn't understand some of that because you're going fast. Could you explain it again?"*
Teacher:	*(Sigh) "I'm going fast because this is a review and you should already know this stuff. I can't go back and reteach you everything you should have learned before. It's not fair to punish everyone because you can't remember what you already learned."*

Sienna's hypervigilance leads her to focus on observing the reactions on several students' faces after each of the teacher's comments. Sienna senses some distress from the other students and can tell the teacher's sarcastic nature is not appropriate, since it is not being received well. She notices the physical signs in her body in reaction to what is going on and feels her anxiety level rising. Sienna has been learning from her counselor how to become more aware of her body and has practiced being intentional about physically distancing herself from any trigger of anxiety until she feels okay. Sienna does not feel safe enough to say anything to the teacher based on all the interactions she has observed so far, as she does not want to put herself in a position to receive negative responses from the teacher and draw attention to herself. She decides to stand up and move toward an empty space in the back of the room to do some subtle stretches and poses in order to self-regulate and get her body back to calm. Sienna tries not to distract other students in the class as she walks to the back of the room, and midway, the teacher yells out to engage in the following conversation in a patronizing manner:

Teacher:	*"What are you doing?"*
Sienna:	*"I'm walking to the back of the class to take a short break and stretch."*
Teacher:	*"Why?"*
Sienna:	*"Because it helps me focus."*
Teacher:	*"You're not allowed to get up out of your seat unless you ask."*
Sienna:	*"Sorry, I didn't know that was a rule."*
Teacher:	*"Well now you know. Go sit down."*
Sienna:	*"I didn't think to ask because we don't have to ask permission to go to the bathroom."*
Teacher:	*"Don't talk back to me. You obviously weren't going to the bathroom, since the door is the other way. The next time you break the rules, you'll have consequences."*

DISCUSSION QUESTIONS

1. What are some aspects about this class environment that seem safe or unsafe?
2. If it was the middle of the school year and the teacher had already built trust with the students, how do you think they might respond to the teacher?
3. How do you think Sienna perceives the school if this class is her first impression?
4. What are some things about this class that might be triggering for Sienna based on her previous school experience?
5. If you were Sienna's parent and she shared what happened with you over dinner that night, what would you do?
6. As a staff member, if you were walking by the classroom and overheard the way the teacher was interacting with students, would you take any action? Why or why not? Would it make a difference if the teacher was one of your friends at work?

Chapter Summary

Providing school climates that focus on physical and emotional safety is necessary for trauma-informed practice, as it fosters calm brains that enable students to engage in meaningful learning processes. Awareness of our own approaches with students, families, and colleagues can help with our development toward becoming more in tune with others and ensure our practices are not creating retraumatizing experiences for students who may or may not have trauma histories. Relationships are the vehicle toward feeling accepted as a valuable part of a school community, and it starts with how we treat each other, even during the smallest moments in our daily interactions. Offering students an environment of safety in which they feel genuine care and connection with us requires our own wellness to be intact to be able to make the best decisions when dealing with difficult situations. Mindfulness, social-emotional learning, and movement/yoga practices are tools students can learn and use to help reduce barriers to learning and disrupt patterns in which they may feel stuck and outside their windows of tolerance. To maintain authenticity when teaching these topics, it is essential for adults in schools to intentionally incorporate some tools—such as mindful awareness, breathing exercises, and presence—into their own wellness tool kits so they can be modeled for students. Self-care practices are cultivated over time, and pathways of healing for students start with the adults taking care of them.

Connect and Reflect

Work in groups as school faculty teams and collaborate on the selected sample questions to consider for preparation toward implementing a trauma-informed culture. These questions have been adapted from SAMHSA (2014) to correspond with relevance to K–12 school environments.

1. How can our school's physical environment promote a sense of safety, calm, and de-escalation for students and staff?
2. In what ways can staff members recognize and address aspects of the physical environment that may be retraumatizing for students?
3. What can the school do to provide space to ensure that staff and students have opportunities to practice self-care?
4. How can transparency and trust among staff and students be promoted?
5. What can the school do to support gender-related physical and emotional safety concerns? Consider gender-specific directives and spaces.
6. How can staff members work to minimize feelings of fear or shame for students?
7. What strategies and processes can the school use to evaluate whether staff members feel safe and valued by the school leadership team and district?

Extended Learning

Duckworth, A. (2016). *Grit: The power of passion and perseverance.* New York, NY: Scribner.

Hawn, G. (2011). *10 mindful minutes: Giving our children—and ourselves—the social and emotional skills to reduce stress and anxiety for healthier, happier lives.* New York, NY: Penguin Group.

Kabat-Zinn, J. (2013). *Full catastrophe living (revised edition): Using the wisdom of your body and mind to face stress, pain, and illness.* New York, NY: Bantam Books.

Siegel, D. (2018). *Aware: The science and practice of presence.* New York, NY: Penguin Random House.

Souers, K., & Hall, P. (2016). *Fostering resilient learners: Strategies for creating a trauma-sensitive classroom.* Alexandria, VA: ASCD.

Credit

Chapter 7

Developing Trauma-Informed Approaches in Schools

THE KNOWLEDGE WE have gained in learning about trauma, brain processes, attachment, childhood adversity, trauma-induced behaviors, safety, wellness, and other topics helps us develop our **trauma lens**, which allows us to recognize and understand students in a new light by supporting a paradigm shift toward a "culture that sustains trauma-sensitive ways of thinking and acting" (Cole et al., 2013, p. 8). This chapter does not provide specific implementation procedures with detailed sample forms and documents, as that process is better suited for school and district leadership teams that involve consistent and intentional collaborative planning with colleagues about what which type of flexible framework would be best for meeting the needs of their student populations and environments. Instead, this chapter will introduce you to a number of topics that are thoughtfully considered by many schools in preparation for transition toward a trauma-informed culture. The objective of such a worthwhile transformation should not be seen merely as a "quick fix" or an additional feature to include on one's resume. This long-term process requires much planning, reflection, collaboration, intention, patience, and investment in becoming truly authentic as a school community.

Trauma impacts students and the adults who care for them. There is no guarantee we will always know if a student's challenges with behaviors, academics, and relationships are related to trauma in a school setting (Cole et al., 2005). Sometimes it may even be inappropriate for school staff members to have knowledge of intimate details surrounding a student's trauma history, as confidentiality is a professional standard that prevents possible harm to the dignity, welfare, and reputation of the student or family (Cole et al., 2013).

Learning Objectives

1. What are the different levels of mindsets included in the spectrum of trauma practices?
2. How can educators help create trauma-informed cultures in their schools and classrooms?
3. What is a *flexible framework* for trauma-informed approaches?
4. What are some positive strategies for fostering a safe, structured, and respectful classroom?
5. What are some differences between traditional forms of discipline and restorative discipline practices?
6. Why is social-emotional learning necessary for trauma-informed practices?
7. What prevention efforts can be implemented to address trauma and ACEs?

For example, assuming entitlement to confidential information that can possibly be used negatively against the student in future interactions, in making educational decisions about the child, or while socializing with colleagues can create disharmony and mistrust within the school community. School staff members may engage in retraumatizing practices due to lack of proper trauma-informed training. According to Perry (2006), "what doesn't work is well intentioned but poorly trained mental health 'professionals' rushing in after a traumatic event, or coercing children to 'open up' or 'get out their anger'" (p. 232). Putting children in an uncomfortable position where they feel forced to comply with what adults think they need is a harmful disservice to the children, as it can foster stronger distrust of adults and model disrespect. Evans and Vaandering (2016) explain: "When power is employed in self-serving ways, relationships are diminished because others are used as objects to further the well-being or success of self" (p. 62). Students can learn how to use power positively instead of trying to have power over others if it is modeled by adults in the school, which requires *us* to learn positive ways to model and teach respectful behavior (Nelsen, 2000).

There are many different aspects of a traumatic experience that could impact how a child might respond, such as age, type of stressful experience, support from family and community, etc. Since the same trauma-inducing event does not affect different children in exactly the same way, it is crucial for all adults in a school to be able to recognize and continue to learn the many ways to respond to the impacts of trauma in schools. Taking steps to move toward a trauma-informed culture in which all staff members are aware of the impacts of trauma can help in providing appropriate support to minimize the negative effects on students, even those who have not yet been recognized as having trauma histories.

Schoolwide Practices

As you continue to enhance your knowledge about trauma, you will notice variations in how schools and organizations describe the level of practices associated with supporting trauma needs in their specific environments. Some school climates that "avoid, overlook, or misunderstand the impact of trauma may often be retraumatizing and interfere with the healing process. Individuals can be retraumatized by the very people whose intent is to be helpful" (Substance Abuse and Mental Health Services Administration, 2014, p. 17). Cole et al. (2013) suggest "the best approach is to make sure we provide trauma-sensitive learning environments for *all* children," (p. 9) which is a component that is consistently emphasized in various programs and approaches supporting trauma-informed practices. Sours and Hall (2019) encourage schools to be reflective, intentional, and authentic in understanding where they currently stand so future goals can align with the needs of the school and suggest that "We need to look at our levels of safety and at the predictability and consistency of our practices to ensure that we really are what we say we are" (p. 23). In Figure 7.1, Sours and Hall (2019) developed a chart labeling the range of trauma-based practices. The brief descriptions of each level are extremely helpful for understanding the differences among the terms, as they can mistakenly be used interchangeably.

	Trauma-Ignorant	Trauma-Aware	Trauma-Sensitive
Trauma-Inducing	Trauma-Indifferent	Trauma-Informed	Trauma-Invested

	Trauma-Inducing	**Trauma-Indifferent**	**Trauma-Informed**	**Trauma-Invested**
Definition	A setting that not only lacks safety but also is actively unsafe for students and/or adults.	A setting that does not take childhood trauma into consideration in its policies and practices.	A setting where stakeholders have acquired some knowledge about childhood trauma and are versed in related strategies.	A setting where stakeholders have consented to act on their knowledge, truly working together to enhance safety across the board.
Behavioral focus	Students are publicly shamed for misbehaviors, triggered intentionally to prompt removal, and embarrassed for their inability to conform.	Discipline practices address behaviors only, without acknowledging what might be causing disruptions.	Trauma-based strategies are used intermittently across settings, including positive reinforcement and safe social and emotional learning (SEL) approaches.	Expectations are clear and adults partner with students to help them safely navigate ways to experience success.
Academic focus	Grading is punitive, students are not given multiple chances to show their growth, and students are neither engaged nor challenged.	Teachers display a lack of flexibility in reaching individual students, and the academic focus overwhelms the whole child approach.	The whole child tenets (healthy, safe, engaged, supported, and challenged) are taken into consideration fairly consistently.	Staff are flexible and adaptable, ensuring opportunities for *each and every* child to be successful as a learner through whole child approaches.
Attendance focus	There is no effort to encourage students to come to school. Their absence is not the school's problem.	Student attendance is recorded.	Student attendance is monitored and students are encouraged to attend school.	Adults partner with students and families to welcome and invite them to school. All commit to increasing attendance.
Relationship focus	Staff overtly show disdain or indifference toward students as human beings. Minimal effort is made toward building relationships with students.	The focus is on academics, test scores, and the business of education rather than relationships.	Many staff members value relationships and understand the importance of connecting with students on a personal level.	Adults ensure that every child has a meaningful champion in the setting, emphasizing relationships as a conduit to learning.

FIGURE 7.1. Spectrum of Trauma Practices; Sours and Hall (2019) (*Continued*)

FIGURE 7.1. (*Continued*)

	Trauma-Inducing	Trauma-Indifferent	Trauma-Informed	Trauma-Invested
Responsibility focus	Student behaviors are viewed through the lens of "will/won't" rather than "can/can't." Staff base determinations about students' potential to learn and succeed on preconceived ideas. Staff take students' choices and behaviors personally, and the way they communicate and interact with students may contribute to students' lack of self-worth.	Student behaviors are often viewed through the lens of "will/won't" rather than "can/can't." Staff jump in to rescue students at the slightest sign of struggle. Staff typically see 70 percent of students as having potential and don't view themselves as a resource or support for the remaining 30 percent. Staff see their roles as solely academic and view the development of responsibility as students' job.	Many students view challenges as opportunities for growth. The growth mindset is prevalent among both staff and students. Staff encourage students to try new things and to own their successes and struggles. Staff believe all students have potential and work to help students achieve their best.	Adults create safe spaces where students can learn, struggle, fail, persevere, and eventually succeed. Staff embolden and encourage students to tackle any task they desire. Staff partner with students and empower them to want to do better. Staff work hard to help improve students' sense of self-worth and belief in themselves.
Regulation focus	Staff react to dysregulated students with frustration, anger, and irritation. It's not safe for students to show their true emotions, so they may try to hide them from adults.	Students have no safe outlet for their emotional responses to life's uncertainties. Staff act according to the belief that students should "pull themselves up by their bootstraps."	Staff understand the need for brain breaks and choice yet still may have trouble being available for students while also holding them accountable for their behaviors. Staff recognize that students can't learn if they aren't regulated and work toward creating safe environments conducive to learning.	Students have multiple options for regulating, and staff have taught them appropriate times and ways to access them. Students have been taught to communicate their needs effectively and healthy ways to regulate so they can learn. All stakeholders agree to fostering a safe environment where students can get into—and stay in—their upstairs brains.

(*Continued*)

	Trauma-Inducing	Trauma-Indifferent	Trauma-Informed	Trauma-Invested
Other descriptors	Adults rely on the exit strategy and are not committed to the whole child.	Adults may or may not know important information (name, interests, goals) about individual students.	There is a movement afoot to learn more about childhood trauma and what can be done to help students be successful.	The whole team is committed to incorporating these practices into the work place for every student.
Words and phrases you might hear	• Failure • Lost cause • Worthless • Waste of time • Not my responsibility • Why bother? • Chaos • Never/always	• Scores first • I have to cover the curriculum • Don't have time • Struggles • That's the counselor's job • This is how we've always done it • Sometimes	• Childhood trauma • Regulation • Relationships • Responsibility • Potential • Strengths • Competing demands • Goals • SEL strategies • Safe enough, healthy enough	• Whole child • Differentiation • Success • Let's work together • I'm here for you • Flexibility • Collaboration • Partnerships • Nest • Safety for all • Connection • Consistency in practice • Predictability
Mindset needed to move forward	First, do no harm.	Gain awareness and learn as much as you can.	Be intentional and implement your knowledge.	Collaborate often and refine your practices.

SELF-CHECK

After reviewing Figure 7.1, decide where would you place yourself on the spectrum. What about before you started reading this book and learning about childhood trauma? Take another look at the section titled "Words and phrases you might hear." Do you have any experiences working at school sites or in other caregiving settings that demonstrate practices along this spectrum?

We learned in Chapter 1 what a trauma-informed approach is, as described by SAMHSA. Schools that incorporate trauma-informed practices have the flexibility of collaborating about which practices would align with the needs of their particular student populations. As you can see from Figure 7.1, a trauma-informed approach encompasses some acquired knowledge and encourages practices for creating strong buy-in from a majority of staff members, which leaves room for momentum toward a future shift in becoming trauma sensitive. Regardless of where a school community may fall on the spectrum of trauma approaches, there will always be room for continuous adjustments along the way toward the goal of becoming trauma invested. Sours and Hall (2019) explain that a trauma-invested approach is a philosophy by which

> we are committing to the belief that all students have potential and are cognizant of how stress can disrupt learning and achievement. We create an environment of safety knowing that trauma is a possibility and aware that this may be the *only* safe space for students to truly learn and thrive. We unite as a team and encourage one another to see the good in others and to offer grace as needed for student success. (p. 27)

Additionally, Cole et al. (2013) developed the following definition to maintain a shared vision of the goals of supporting students struggling with trauma:

> A trauma-sensitive school is one in which all students feel safe, welcomed, and supported and where addressing trauma's impact on learning on a school-wide basis is at the center of its educational mission. An ongoing, inquiry-based process allows for the necessary teamwork, coordination, creativity, and sharing of responsibility for all students. (p. 11)

Cole et al. (2013) also developed the following six core attributes to embrace a trauma-sensitive school approach:

1. Leadership and staff share an understanding of trauma's impact on learning and the need for a school-wide approach.
2. The school supports all students to feel safe physically, socially, emotionally, and academically.
3. The school addresses students' needs in holistic ways, taking into account their relationships, self-regulation, academic competence, and physical and emotional health and well-being.
4. The school explicitly connects students to the school community and provides multiple opportunities to practice newly developing skills.
5. The school embraces teamwork, and staff share responsibility for all students.
6. Leadership and staff anticipate and adapt to the ever-changing needs and the surrounding community. (pp. 18–26)

SELF-CHECK

If you just accepted a job at a school that was in the process of moving forward from being trauma informed to becoming trauma sensitive, what would be some potential barriers to implementing any of the six core attributes above?

In efforts to collaborate and plan to ensure a school is ready for moving toward a trauma-sensitive culture, it is necessary for leadership teams to carefully consider several factors that may fuel or hinder the motivation toward change. The "Flexible Framework" provides guidelines for schoolwide practices, is intended to be adaptable to any school community, and is introduced briefly below, as your familiarity with these six elements may benefit you as a current or future professional in a school that is implementing trauma-informed practices (Cole et al., 2013):

1.   Leadership by school and district administrators to create the infrastructure and culture
2.   Professional development and skill building for all school staff
3.   Access to resources and services, such as mental health and other resources, that help students participate fully in the school community
4.   Academic and nonacademic strategies that enable all children to learn
5.   Policies, procedures, and protocols that sustain the critical elements
6.   Collaboration with families (p. 27)

If you are interested in deeper learning about the Flexible Framework, see the "Extended Learning" section at the end of this chapter for additional resources.

Cultural Awareness

Best practices for a trauma-informed culture incorporate culturally responsive teaching practices that are necessary for working with students with histories of adversity and trauma. **Culturally responsive teaching** uses positive and constructive instructional strategies that affirm students' cultural displays of learning and meaning-making in the learning environment. Incorporating a relational approach to the role of teaching helps to build meaningful connections with students and contributes to a safe learning environment (Hammond, 2015). Romero, Robertson, and Warner (2018) maintain:

> Culturally responsive teaching affirms and welcomes all our students and all that makes them who they are. This approach to teaching breaks down the isolating and alienating effects of ACEs, trauma, and marginalization, giving students the opportunity to share their experiences, feelings, and histories. When young people feel heard, validated, and valued, there is an opportunity for healing. Inclusive curriculum, culturally responsive teaching, positive behavioral interventions, and restorative practices mitigate the impact of trauma in our classrooms. Individually, we may not be able to change the world, but we have the power to create classroom communities that offer refuge and foster resilience. (p. 50)

It is necessary for trauma-informed practices to strive for equitable outcomes in order to best support students struggling with trauma. Understanding how the brain responds and interacts with others is necessary for a culturally responsive educator (Hammond, 2015). We learned in Chapter 4 that trauma can emerge from historical and generational contexts, as the "emotional and psychological impact of genocide, enslavement, cultural erasure, forced removal from land, extreme poverty, and long-term abuse can be passed on from generation to generation" (Romero, Robertson, & Warner, 2018, p. 49).

Power of Teachers, Administrators, and School Staff

School communities have the power to create rich social environments for students through conscious decisions to focus on relationships first so that healing and learning can take place. All students, including those without trauma backgrounds, can benefit from safe and connected school cultures. A whole-school approach is inclusive of all students and empowers educators to be ready to intervene in a holistic manner. Every staff member in the school can develop the capacity for providing struggling students with a space to experience the four Ss of attachment (seen, safe, soothed, secure) if they are supported with appropriate professional development, as mentioned in the six elements of the Flexible Framework. Flexibility and open-mindedness are key: "A supportive school-wide environment can play a significant role in addressing the needs of students who have endured traumatic experiences" (Cole et al., 2013, p. 8).

Since barriers can shape reactive behaviors, it can be challenging to overcome staff attitudes driven by unawareness of the need to adapt, resistance to change, systems of oppression and privilege, and a sense of entitlement (Nuri-Robins, Lindsey, Lindsey, & Terrell, 2012). We are failing our children when we fail to see that it is our collective responsibility as adults to do the best we can to make sure every single student feels safe and connected to all adults in the school. Educators and support staff must shift out of the mindset that trauma-related behaviors are deliberate so that potentially retraumatizing disciplinary actions can be avoided (Cole, Eisner, Gregory, & Ristuccia, 2013). Intentional efforts toward building trusting relationships with fellow colleagues helps to foster authentic connections so difficult conversations can take place without shame or blame (Romero, Robertson, & Warner, 2018).

School Counselors and Mental Health Professionals

When students have difficulty articulating their needs or expressing themselves appropriately in school settings, school counselors, social workers, and other mental health professionals are excellent resources trained in utilizing various appropriate methods for communicating with dysregulated students. The school counselor serves as a consultant for teachers to collaborate with and learn appropriate strategies from, as building relationships is at the core of their role and identity within the school community. It is vital for school counselors to enter the profession informed and equipped with quality training so they can feel confident enough to tackle the range of student issues associated with trauma and be adequately prepared to consult, support, intervene, and collaborate with colleagues. Because the school counselor is a specially trained professional, it is essential for their skills, time, and work with students to be respected and trusted by the staff in order to prevent possibly jeopardizing decision-making skills or student/family needs and privacy. School counselors often struggle with the difficult task of attempting to connect regularly with every single student in the school or in their caseloads because much of their time may be dedicated to the few students with extremely high needs in addition to several other administrative duties they are obligated to fulfill. Various administrative tasks that cause school counselors to step away from focusing on the main duties associated with their role can lead to increased unavailability to students to provide the very services they are specially trained to do.

School counselors are often the recipients of student referrals associated with negative behavior, with an assumption that school counselors can facilitate "quick fixes" for troubled students as the only alternative to punishments. This perspective supports a deficit mindset by implying that students are "broken," which is the complete opposite philosophy of a trauma-informed culture. Perry (2006) explains: "What maltreated and traumatized children most need is a healthy community to buffer the pain, distress, and loss caused by their earlier trauma. What works to heal them is anything that increases the number and quality of a child's relationships" (p. 232). With increased caseloads, rising student needs, and extra administrative duties, a school counselor often holds the extra weight of being the only trained professional in the school who is able to deliver trauma-informed approaches. Due to the rising recognition of trauma and escalating needs of many students that faculty and staff are faced with, it can be beneficial for schools to shift school counselors, social workers, and school psychologists away from being the sole stewards of mental health toward schoolwide approaches that encompass awareness, connectedness, and prevention. In a trauma-informed culture, all staff members have roles in offering students a safe haven through their way of being.

School counselors, social workers, and other school-based mental health professionals at school and district levels can collaborate with administration and take the lead in delivering or coordinating ongoing professional development opportunities for teachers about how to integrate social-emotional curriculum into daily classroom practices (Romero, Robertson, & Warner, 2018). All staff members in the school who interact with students, such as front office administration, bus drivers, cafeteria employees, maintenance staff, etc., can receive training that includes topics related to brain science, stress, trauma, building student relationships, and staff wellness. Romero, Robertson, and Warner (2018) recommend that when school leadership teams begin focusing on the transition to a trauma-informed culture, "The first steps are to make sure all staff members, administrators, teachers, nurses, school counselors, and cafeteria and custodial staff understand the need and are prepared for the transformation" (p. 64).

Administrators

Research conducted by Abel, Eggleston, Green, and Poe (2018) provides a guide for school principals titled *Lessons Learned*, which is composed of several key points that serve as valuable reminders as planning is carried out toward the goal of become trauma aware. Although it is specifically designated for principals, other school administrators and professionals who may serve on leadership teams, such as the assistant principal, school counselor, school-based social worker, and grade-level coordinators, could also benefit from reviewing the guide below for reflection purposes as planning and collaboration continues. The guide states that *principals must realize*:

- they are ultimately responsible for leading trauma awareness in their schools;
- the urgency for their staff and leaders to become trauma aware;
- the prevalence and impact of childhood trauma specifically within their school community;
- students who are impacted by trauma exist in every school;
- trauma affects every age, race, ethnicity, gender, and socioeconomic level;
- childhood trauma impacts student learning and behavior;
- students cannot perform academically or pass standardized tests if they are not emotionally self-regulated;
- the value of engaging families and community members in the process of becoming trauma aware;
- trauma awareness introduces a fundamental change of mindset from punitive to restorative discipline;
- trauma awareness promotes equity;
- equity demands a focus on the whole child;
- the need to create a sense of urgency and build a guiding coalition for trauma awareness;
- the guiding coalition should include as many types of stakeholders as possible, including students at the secondary level. (p. 69)

Additionally, it is beneficial for school leaders to understand that "Teachers work smarter and more efficiently in systems that honor their professional expertise and provide continuous professional development opportunities and in school environments that are emotionally safe and supporting" (Romero, Robertson, & Warner, 2018, p. 61).

Teachers and Support Staff

When school environments neglect focusing on the whole student in order to put the focus on assessments and testing, staff members may continue to deal with elevated stress levels without any supports in place for self-care. It is no wonder that some teachers strongly feel they cannot attend to investing their time into getting to know their students and building relationships. They themselves are not afforded the calm and patience necessary to do so because of the overwhelming demands that force the creativity and passion of teaching to wither away from their identities as educators. The domino effect of this includes stressed-out teachers without capacity to support students, punitive responses assigned by these stressed-out teachers, and increased student referrals to school counselors and administration. If teachers desire a change in their current school climates for their own wellness and health of their students, an urgency to advocate can "contribute to the process of building a trauma-informed culture by offering their voice in planning professional development needs" (Romero, Robertson, & Warner, p. 75) and other schoolwide practices supporting such a shift.

An educator's consistent interest in each student on a daily basis is crucial for establishing personal quality relationships and serves as a buffer against the negative impacts of at-risk students (Rak & Patterson, 1996). Trauma-informed approaches emphasize inclusion of all support staff—such as specialists, paraprofessionals, cafeteria employees, bus drivers, maintenance staff, school nurses, and administrative professionals—in serving as protective buffers contributing to student success and resiliency.

It is difficult to see trauma without a trauma lens, and this can lead to reinforcing negative patterns of punishing students for behaviors indicative of trauma. There are several ways for teachers to successfully create safe and equitable classrooms to ensure students are getting what they need to be able to learn. The following list provides examples of some of the many positive strategies for fostering a safe, structured, and respectful classroom for students who may be struggling with trauma histories (Echo, 2017a, 2017b, 2017c; Romero, Robertson, & Warner, 2018; Smith & Lambert, 2008):

- Build trusting and connected relationships with students—follow through with promises and be honest and transparent when changes are unavoidable
- Have a calming corner used as quiet space for students to decompress if they are feeling overwhelmed (this should not be stigmatized as a "time out" space)
- Offer choices so students may have a sense of control and avoid power struggles
- Predictability and routines that prepare students for transitions can create a sense of safety
- Incorporate social-emotional learning into classroom activities—many sample resources are provided in the next practice exercise
- Assume each student carries with them an invisible contract that states, "Please teach me appropriate behavior in a safe and structured environment"
- Monitor your volume, tone, and posture for appropriateness and maintain a calm and pleasant attitude (refrain from humiliating students in front of their peers)
- Two by Ten (2·10) Strategy—for your most challenging students, have personal conversations about anything the student is interested in (appropriate topics) for 2 minutes each day, 10 days in a row
- Classroom acknowledgment circles or class meetings
- Greet students each morning at the door or have a different student greet peers at the door each morning
- Handshakes unique to each student to show value and belonging
- Break one-step instructions down into multiple steps to ensure successful completion of tasks (instead of "Get ready for recess," guide with multiple steps, such as "Close your books and put them back on the shelf; put your worksheet and pencil inside your desk; push your chairs in; put on your sweater or jacket; line up at the door.")
- Use visuals to help clarify expectations using an Activboard or overhead projector (pictures of a clean desk or lunch table or pictures of all required materials for the next activity)

Discipline

We learned in Chapter 1 that the fourth key assumption of a trauma-informed approach is to resist retraumatization of staff and students. School staff members can often unknowingly create highly stressful or toxic disciplinary consequences that trigger painful experiences for students with trauma backgrounds (Substance Abuse and Mental Health Services Administration, 2014). Best practices using a trauma-informed lens consider the impacts of trauma and adverse experiences on a student's behavior and home life when considering disciplinary actions, as the focus should be on the safety of every member of the school environment, appropriate support services, and use of restorative discipline practices (National Child Traumatic Stress Network, Schools Committee, 2017). **Restorative discipline practices** recognize that:

> Because schools are educational institutions, the school's response to children's behavior should be consistent with education's goals of supporting teaching and learning—not punishment, retribution, and exclusion. From the individual child's perspective, the school is acknowledged as a social community where every child belongs and where children's behavioral challenges are addressed through supportive educational interventions. From a whole-school perspective, restorative practices have the development of positive relationships and peaceful resolution of conflict for staff and students as their primary aims. (Meyer & Evans, 2012, pp. 5–6)

The main components of restorative school discipline practices include a "focus on relationships; problem solving; the prevention and peaceful resolution of conflict; and strategies for restoration and making amends where harm has occurred" (Meyer & Evans, 2012, p. 18). Since restorative practices are not a behavior management system and strongly consider the relational context, "school-based relationships should be characterized by justice and equity … designed to facilitate relationships in which everyone is treated with worth and dignity" (Evans & Vaandering, 2016, p. 50) within an inclusive school climate. **Equity** is defined as fairness or impartiality to ensure each individual gets what they need in order to experience well-being (Evans & Vaandering, 2016). *Equal* does not mean the same thing as *equity*, as they are often mistakenly used interchangeably. If all students are being treated the same or equally, some students may not be getting what they need to be successful. This may be difficult for school staff members and students to grasp, as a common complaint about attempting to transition into such practices is that there are no consequences for student behavior. The three essential elements that characterize restorative school cultures are (Evans & Vaandering, 2016):

1. Creating just and equitable learning environments: Each member of the school community is accepted for who they are. All aspects of the school culture represent justice and equity as respectfully meeting student needs and not as equal distribution of resources.

2. Nurturing healthy relationships: Social and emotional development are essential for learning. All components of the educational climate integrate aspects of healthy connections, such as respect, inclusion, conflict resolution, reciprocal learning, and teaching,

3. Repairing harm and transforming conflict: Experiencing conflict and harm is a normal part of life and provides learning opportunities and possibility for personal transformation.

Meyers and Evans (2012) explain that "restorative school discipline is people focused, accepting that positive and supportive relationships are crucial for learning to occur in educational environments so that conflict must be addressed by making amends where relationships will otherwise be damaged and even broken" (p. 7). Focusing on student strengths fosters attitudes toward resiliency that enable us to treat both our students and ourselves with respect and dignity. It helps us understand that when students act out, they are sending us a message that they want a positive connection. Then we can start to see "discipline moments" as opportunities for teaching an essential piece that students want to learn (Smith & Lambert, 2008). Supporting the recovery of students with trauma backgrounds requires even more routines and repetition due to the fact that learning and neuroplasticity are activated by consistent and patterned experiences. Time and patience are core requirements of practices utilized by school staff members because "the longer the period of trauma, or the more extreme the trauma, the greater the number of repetitions required to regain balance" (Perry, 2006, p. 245).

Practicing trauma-informed care is more than just not suspending students or not taking them out of class; it is increasing teacher capacity to build resiliency in our students. To have a trauma-informed classroom is the opposite of letting students get away with bad behavior—it is about providing them with the tools and reflection time to correct their behavior and regulate their minds and bodies. It is about providing routines, predictability, and structure in their worlds, which are often built on chaos and unpredictability. It is about providing them love and support in a world that can be full of criticism and hopelessness. It is about providing them a safe and comfortable environment they can rely on. The more we expect of our students in a nurturing climate, the more they will thrive. Structure and high expectations in a supportive environment build the self-worth and confidence many students with chronic stress desperately desire and need (Starr Commonwealth, 2019).

Developing teacher capacity for trauma-informed approaches includes building relationships with students, intentional curiosity about student behavior, understanding that student behavior is not personal, and recognizing that it does not signify that students are *getting away* with unacceptable behavior (Starr Commonwealth, 2019). Nelsen, Lott, and Glenn (2000) describe how some adults expect students to quickly acquire "wisdom and sound judgment without the opportunity to practice, make mistakes, learn, and try again" (p. 17) and that children can develop good decision-making skills when we provide "opportunities and encouragement to make choices and decisions in an environment that emphasizes learning from mistakes instead of paying for mistakes through some kind of punishment" (Nelsen, Lott, & Glenn, 2000, p. 16).

Burke Harris (2018) discusses how the origin of many disruptive behaviors in different students struggling with trauma is attributed to the chronic stress and lack of safety they sense regularly in their lives, such as living in communities of violence, bullying at school, bullying outside of school through social media, unforgiving and demanding caregivers who emotionally harm or neglect them, etc. We learned from Chapter 1 how traditional methods of discipline characterized by reactive and punitive consequences result in many costs to the welfare of the student, including loss of significant learning time in the classroom and damaged self-esteem. Burke Harris (2018) explains:

> In order to be able to pay attention and learn in school, a kid needed to engage his pre-frontal cortex (the conductor), which meant the amygdala alarm had to be silent. Safety and stability would be key components to the solution ... many of the kids they were serving, the amygdala alarm was always on high alert, and the cortisol thermostat was overheating. ... The natural antidote to toxic stress—having a well-regulated caregiver who could buffer the stress response—was often in very short supply. (p. 185)

When a student shows us that they are having a difficult time through their behaviors, school staff members dealing with such situations may often resort to a default method of immediately talking to the student about what they are doing wrong and what the student should do or should have done to prevent the behaviors. Just as Siegel (2011) describes in *The Whole Brain Child*, it is necessary to focus first on the dysregulated stress-response system and bring it back down to calm before attempting to problem solve. For example, if you do not know how to swim and a lifeguard notices you are struggling and might be drowning in the ocean, the lifeguard will probably rush to reach you and then try to get you back to dry land. Imagine that when the lifeguard finally reaches you and your stress-response system is going haywire, the lifeguard asks you, "Why did you do that? What should you have done to avoid this? You need to make better choices." Would that calm your amygdala in the moment? These reflective questions require access to the PFC, or upstairs brain, which you would not have access to as you are frantically trying not to drown. Your stress-response system at that moment is no different from the stress-response system of a child who senses extreme danger, regardless of what the root or trigger is. Siegel's video, *Connecting to Calm* from Chapter 2, is a great resource that reminds us of what this sequencing can look like.

A respectful and caring school environment that encourages optimal learning takes the necessary steps to exclude practices that embody humiliation and punishment (Nelsen, 2000). For many students suffering from trauma, it is important to recognize they may need to establish basic groundwork in healthy relationships and attachment, stress management, and self-regulation (Burke Harris, 2018). Reserving a safe, private place for students to retreat to for quiet reflection while tuning in to what is going on in their bodies is a much better alternative than allowing a triggered student to escalate into an inappropriate outburst in the presence of their peers and school staff. Maintaining a student's dignity and privacy within the school community should be one of the top priorities when helping a student who is having a difficult moment. It is also important to continue a respectful approach when considering next steps after an incident and to maintain professionalism when staff or other students prompt a discussion about it.

How would you react if you came home after a long day of learning, studying, and/or working and you were told that you are not allowed to decompress or do whatever you want with your time? While you yearn for certain ways to help you relax, you are required to keep working or studying without breaks and cannot chat with your friends or family. Your experience of what this could feel like may be similar for students who are expected to spend most of their school days learning in the classroom without adequate time for mental breaks or valuable socializing and unstructured play with peers. Think about how punishing a student by preventing him of her from joining recess with their peers can be like telling you that you are not allowed to go exercise with your friends. Additionally, if that student is in trouble for not being able to sit still and focus, opportunities to release excess energy and regulate them back to calm are being taken away. The strategy for trying to teach that student to calm down in class is actually working against the very person who is assigning it, which can make it increasingly difficult for adults to develop trusting relationships with students. Continuously keeping a student from having recess and socializing or attending classes they enjoy (art, physical education, etc.) as a consequence of unfinished work can be similar to telling you that you cannot take breaks to practice self-care. As adults, our fully (or almost fully) developed brains allow us to sustain higher levels of self-discipline than our student's brains do for them; however, these types of consequences take away necessary opportunities for social-emotional development and practicing emotional regulation. According to Walkley and Cox (2013), "Significant reduction in discipline issues is one of the positive outcomes noted when school leadership, despite challenges in implementation, commits to a change in school climate and culture through trauma-informed approaches" (p. 125).

SELF-CHECK

How were you or your peers disciplined during your childhood? Was it helpful in changing your future behavior? What are some discipline techniques that worked or did not work in "teaching you a lesson"?

Practice #1

Below is a list of resources that would be helpful for leadership teams to explore when planning and developing schoolwide trauma-informed supports and practices. This list includes resources for social-emotional learning, discipline, self-care, restorative practices, and schoolwide implementation programs. It was compiled from several resources and is in no way exhaustive, as there are plentiful excellent resources that currently exist and that continue to be developed. Lightly research each resource below with a group or on your own and make brief notes about each one. This activity will help you become familiar with the types of programs and classroom practices that are already embedded in some school cultures. Then answer the following question:

If your school principal or district supervisor distributed this list to school staff and surveyed everyone about the top three choices they would consider for transitioning into a trauma-informed school, which three would you choose? Why? If you worked in a group, you may choose three resources as a group.

Trauma-Informed Resources

1. Starr Commonwealth: https://starr.org/trauma-informed-care-in-a-school-setting/
2. Sanctuary Model by Dr. Sandra L. Bloom: sanctuaryweb.com
3. CLEAR (Collaborative Learning for Educational Achievement and Resilience): extension.wsu/clear/about/
4. Compassionate Schools Project: www.compassionschools.org
5. HEARTS (Healthy Environments and Response to Trauma in Schools): hearts.ucsf.edu
6. CASEL (Collaborative for Academic, Social, and Emotional Learning): casel.org
7. Handle With Care: Michigan Initiative: handlewithcaremi.org
8. CAPPD (Calm, Attuned, Present, Predictable, Don't let the child's emotions escalate your own): www.multiplyingconnections.org/become-trauma-informed/cappd-interventions-guide
9. Making SPACE for Learning: professionals.childhood.org.au/about/
10. Turnaround for Children: turnaroundusa.org/
11. Mindful Schools: www.mindfulschools.org
12. Caring Schools Community: www.collaborativeclassroom.org/programs/caring-school-community
13. MindUp Curriculum: mindup.org
14. Fix School Discipline: www.fixschooldiscipline.org
15. Neurosequential Model: www.neurosequential.com
16. Zones of Regulation: www.zonesofregulation.com
17. Circle Forward: www.circleforward.us/what-is-circle-forward
18. Conscious Discipline: consciousdiscipline.com
19. Holistic Life Foundation: hlfinc.org
20. Go Noodle: www.gonoodle.com
21. Second Step Curriculum: www.secondstep.org
22. Move This World: movethisworld.com

Prevention Through Education and Connection

Schools and communities around the nation and the world are increasingly joining the movement to promote education and awareness about childhood trauma. Continued assumptions that trauma only exists in certain communities only reinforces the shame and resistance against a paradigm shift that require educating individuals and societies about the biological impacts of toxic stress (Burke Harris, 2018). The healing of trauma is dependent on relationships and the reestablishment of trust, loving connection, and a sense of safety (Perry, 2006). As buffering adults, we can take action holistically through our relationships and ways of being; however, one of the main challenges is that "we can't treat what we refuse to see" (Burke Harris, 2018, p. 171).

Many individuals have the capabilities to overcome one or more traumatic experiences and strengthen their resiliency, while others find it difficult to cope while suffering from the overwhelmingly devastating impacts on health (Substance Abuse and Mental Health Services Administration, 2014). Burke Harris explains (2018):

> Toxic stress is a result of a disruption to the stress response. This is a fundamental biological mechanism, not a money problem or a neighborhood problem or a character problem. That means we can look at one another differently. We can see one another as humans with different experiences that have triggered the same physiological response. We can leave the blame and shame out of it and just tackle the problem the same way we would treat any other health condition. (p. 171)

Understanding basic information about how trauma influences a child's neurobiology and functioning can help shape school staff responses to difficult behaviors. Students may benefit from reduced health risk behaviors and social and academic skills in a healthy school environment that models and encourages positive connections (Catalano et al., 2004). Successful changes in individuals, pedagogy, and interpersonal relationships among school staff and students can be carried out through "professional development explaining how change will benefit the adults, first and foremost" (Romero, Robertson, & Warner, 2018, pp. 56–57).

More and more schools can increase awareness about the role of adults when fostering social and emotional competence for children, as it recognizes the need for "greater focus on those interventions and community investments that reduce external threats to healthy brain growth" (Garner et al., 2012, p. e224). Tyler, Allison, and Winslor (2006) recommend that professionals collaborate with parents, the community, and policy officials to raise awareness of childhood trauma and work toward prevention efforts. Anda (2019) notes that a barrier to such collaborative efforts is that "the professions, research priorities, organizations, and resources that are necessary to healing frequently exist in 'silos'—separate, often competitive rather than collaborative, entities, each preserving and advancing the resources and work that is historically 'theirs'" (p. 14). Just as important as the need to disrupt negative patterns of childhood adversity, professionals and caretakers across all sectors must recognize the long-term benefits of working in partnerships in order to "distribute the antidote all over the community because the antidote is safe, stable, and nurturing relationships and environments" (Burke Harris, 2019).

Family and Community Engagement

Parent engagement is a common issue schools face as they strive to increase participation during school events such as open houses, curriculum nights, parent conferences, and themed parent nights. Families may not be able to attend parent events at school due to various reasons, including work obligations, transportation issues, childcare, shame, or lack of trust in the school, and it is important to recognize that building initial trust starts with stepping back from assuming that absent parents are not invested in their child's education or well-being (Abel, Eggleston, Green, & Poe, 2018). It would also be helpful for school professionals to consider the possibility that some families may be struggling from historical, community, or intergenerational trauma. Based on each unique situation, families and their children may very well need the unconditional support of the school, especially if there is a need for access to community resources.

Abel et al. (2018) provide valuable suggestions for professional communication and building positive relationships with parents and caregivers. They are listed below and include examples of dialogue:

PARENT COMMUNICATION

DO NOT:
- **Blame the child** ("I have told John that he needs to stop hitting, but he chooses to keep putting his hands on other kids.")
- **Assume status** ("John's behavior is not appropriate for third grade, and he knows that. Please teach him these behavior expectations at home.")
- **Give attribute praise** ("Your child is smart.")
- **Shame the child** ("John hit someone today, and he isn't sorry about it. He will miss recess today and will be sent to the front office if this happens again.")
- **Use educational jargon** ("John is in Tier 2 for RTI based on SAM data.")

DO:
- **Consider your role** ("I'm working on ways to help John learn to use nice hands. I'd like to discuss the strategies I've been using and get your feedback.")
- **Assume the parent is your partner** ("I know we both want John to be successful, so there are a few behaviors we need to work on to help him be his best.")
- **Give specific examples** ("John takes initiative with problem solving. For example …")
- **Work on a plan with the child and parent** ("John and I had a discussion about hitting other students. Here's what we decided would have been a better choice and how he can fix what he has done. What would you like to add, Mom?")
- **Provide a clear explanation** ("Recent math scores show that John will benefit from a math intervention group.")

Family strength during a positive childhood is a protective factor against the harmful short-term and long-term effects of early adversity and trauma (Anda et al., 2010). Larkin, Felitti, and Anda (2013) explain that "Parents are sometimes presented with problem behaviors or disabilities in their children for which they may not have the knowledge or social support to respond effectively to prevent adverse experiences for their children" (p. 7). Social-emotional learning continues to gain recognition as a necessity in school curriculums for developing basic foundations in successful learning and self-regulation skills, especially for environments that traditionally have maintained heavy and rigorous academic programs while dismissing the significance of addressing social-emotional needs of students. Recommended prevention efforts can focus on educating caregivers, school employees, and other community professionals to promote protective factors that help strengthen families and encourage healthy youth brain development (Child Welfare Information Gateway, Children's Bureau, & FRIENDS National Resource Center for Community-Based Child Abuse Prevention, 2019):

1. Parental resilience
2. Social connections
3. Knowledge of parenting and child/adolescent development
4. Concrete support in times of need
5. Social-emotional competence of children
6. Nurturing and attachment

CASE EXAMPLE

Access the link below and listen to the audio broadcast from National Public Radio about a public elementary school located in Seattle, Washington. You may also read the transcribed article in this link if you desire; however, the audio provides an additional layer of sensory experience that may be helpful when reflecting on the discussion questions.

https://www.kuow.org/stories/district-didnt-want-us-visit-struggling-seattle-school

DISCUSSION QUESTIONS

Work with a partner or group to discuss and answer the following questions:

1. If you were a teacher working in this school, would you treat students differently based on whether or not they had stable housing? Why or why not? If you did not know which students were homeless, do you think you would make assumptions and treat them differently?

2. What are some behaviors or other signs that trauma exists for students at this school? What else indicates this school community is experiencing trauma as a whole?

3. A student in this school asks a teacher for help with a peer conflict, and the teacher responds by saying, "You have to settle it. You're in fourth grade now. You have to do it by yourself." How do you think that student might begin to view the adults in this school? How might this response influence the student's world views as they get older?

4. Based on what you have learned about developing a trauma-informed lens, what healing strategies and skills could you practice immediately to help de-escalate situations or prevent student eruptions from happening?

> ### Reflection
>
> Did you find it easy for you and your group members to discuss these questions? Why or why not? What barriers to collaboration might you expect to encounter if you were having similar discussions with your future colleagues during a faculty meeting?

Chapter Summary

We have an extraordinary opportunity to offer healing to all communities and educational systems impacted by trauma through safe, stable, and nurturing relationships and environments. It is necessary to equip ourselves with the knowledge that enables us to develop a trauma lens in order to work toward implementing effective and respectful restorative practices so every member of the school community benefits. Educators can collaborate about their own level of knowledge, self-care, and needs so professional development opportunities can empower school staff members to support each other in building meaningful relationships with students and becoming buffering adults. Healing of trauma, toxic stress, and childhood adversity starts with the adults, as it is our responsibility to use our trauma lens and take action in disrupting negative cycles so nurturing ways of being can be passed down to future generations.

Connect and Reflect

1. Do you notice any differences in your perspective now in comparison to how you felt before learning about developing a trauma-informed lens?
2. As you progressed through this book, were there times when you struggled or felt uncomfortable with the topics being discussed? Why or why not?
3. In Chapter 1, you were asked to reflect on why you decided to become an educator or work in a school setting. Would you change your answer now that you have been introduced to the value of a trauma-informed culture?
4. Imagine you are at a job interview for a school you highly desire to be employed at. How would you respond if the principal asked you, "What does trauma-informed mean?"
5. What should a school's mission statement include to communicate a commitment to providing a trauma-informed culture?

Extended Learning

Cole, S. F., Eisner, A., Gregory, M., & Ristuccia, J. (2013). *Helping traumatized children learn, volume 2: Creating and advocating trauma-sensitive schools*. Boston, MA: Massachusetts Advocates for Children.

Evans, K., & Vaandering, D. (2016). *The little book of restorative justice in education: Fostering responsibility, healing, and hope in schools*. New York, NY: Good Books.

Hammond, Z. (2015). *Culturally responsive teaching and the brain: Promoting authentic engagement and rigor among culturally and linguistically diverse students*. Thousand Oaks, CA: Corwin.

Meyer, L. H., & Evans, I. M. (2012). *The school leader's guide to restorative discipline*. Thousand Oaks, CA: Corwin.

Nelsen, J., Lott, L., & Glenn, H. S. (2000). *Positive discipline in the classroom: Developing mutual respect, cooperation, and responsibility in your classroom*. New York, NY: Three Rivers Press.

Wolpow, R., Johnson, M. M., Hertel, R., & Kincaid, S. O. (2016). *The heart of learning and teaching: Compassion, resiliency, and academic success* (3rd ed.). Olympia, WA: Washington State Office of Superintendent of Public Instruction Compassionate Schools. Retrieved from http://www.k12.wa.us/compassionateschools/pubdocs/TheHeartofLearningandTeaching.pdf

Credit

References

Abel, S. A., Eggleston, K. B., Green, E. J., & Poe, S. L. (2018). *Becoming a trauma-responsive school: A guide for Virginia leaders*. Richmond, VA: Stop Child Abuse Now.

ACE-Aware Scotland. (2019). *Making Scotland the world's first ACE-aware nation*. Retrieved from http://aceawarescotland.com/ace-aware-2018/

Advancement Project. (2005). *Education on lockdown: The school to jailhouse track*. Washington, DC: Author. Retrieved from https://b.3cdn.net/advancement/5351180e24cb166d02_mlbrqgxlh.pdf

Ainsworth, M. D. S., Blehar, M. C., Waters, E., & Wall, S. (1978*). Patterns of attachment: A psychological study of the strange situation*. Hillsdale, NJ: Lawrence Erlbaum Associates.

Almeida, D. M., Neupert, S. D., Banks, S. R., & Serido, J. (2005). Do daily stress processes account for socioeconomic health disparities? *Journal of Gerontology Series B: Psychological Sciences and Social Sciences, 60*(2), 34–39.

American Bar Association. (2001). *Criminal justice report no. 103B*. Washington, DC: Author. Retrieved from https://www.americanbar.org/content/dam/aba/directories/policy/2001_my_103b.authcheckdam.pdf

American Psychiatric Association. (2013). *Diagnostic and statistical manual of mental disorders* (5th ed.). Washington, DC: Author.

Anda, R. A. (2006, October 19). *The health and social impact of growing up with adverse childhood experiences: The human and economic costs of the status quo*. Paper presented at the National Association for Children of Alcoholics Forum.

Anda, R. F., Dube, S. R., Felitti, V. J., Hills, S. D., Macaluso, M., Marchbanks, P. A., & Marks, J. S. (2010). The protective effect of family strengths in childhood against pregnancy and its long-term psychosocial consequences. *The Permanente Journal, 14*(3), 18–27.

Anderson, L. W., Krathwohl, D. R., Airasian, P. W., Cruikshank, K. A., Mayer, R. E., Pintrich, P. R., Raths, J., & Wittrock, M. C. (2001). *A taxonomy for learning, teaching, and assessing: A revision of Bloom's taxonomy of educational objectives (complete edition)*. New York, NY: Longman.

Babbel, S. (2014). *Compassion fatigue: Bodily symptoms of empathy*. Retrieved from https://www.psychologytoday.com/us/blog/somatic-psychology/201207/compassion-fatigue

Blackburn, E., & Epel, E. (2017). *The telomere effect: A revolutionary approach to living younger, healthier, longer*. New York, NY: Grand Central Publishing.

Bowlby, J. (1973). *Attachment and loss: Vol. 2—Separation*. New York, NY: Basic Books.

Bowlby, J. (1980). *Attachment and loss: Vol. 3—Loss, sadness and depression*. New York, NY: Basic Books.

Bowlby, J. (1982). *Attachment and loss: Vol. 1—Attachment* (2nd ed.). New York, NY: Basic Books.

Burke, N. J., Hellman, J. L., Scott, B. G., Weems, C. F., & Carrion, V. G. (2011). The impact of adverse childhood experiences on an urban pediatric population. *Child Abuse & Neglect, 35*, 408–413. doi:10.1016/j.chiabu.2011.02.006

Burke Harris, N. (2018). *The deepest well: Healing the long-term effects of childhood adversity*. New York, NY: Houghton Mifflin Harcourt.

Burke Harris, N. (2019, April 25). *Keynote speech*. Presented at the VA Summit on Childhood Trauma and Resilience, hosted by Voices for Virginia's Children, Richmond, VA [Video]. Retrieved from https://vakids.org/join-us/events/virginia-summit-on-childhood-trauma-and-resilience

Catalano, R. F., Haggerty, K. P., Oesterle, S., Fleming, C. B., & Hawkins, D. (2004). The importance of bonding to school for healthy development: Findings from the social development research group. *Journal of School Health, 74*(7), 252–261.

Center on the Developing Child. (2019). *Toxic stress.* Cambridge, MA: Harvard University. Retrieved from https://developingchild.harvard.edu/science/key-concepts/toxic-stress/

Chapman, D. P., Dube, S. R., & Anda, R. F. (2007). Adverse childhood events as risk factors for negative mental health outcomes. *Psychiatric Annals, 375*, 359–364. Retrieved from https://www.healio.com/journals/psycann

Charmandari, E., Tsigos, C., & Chrousos, G. (2005). Endocrinology of the stress response. *Annual Review of Physiology, 67*(1), 259–284. doi:10.1146/annurev.physiol.67.040403.120816

Child Welfare Information Gateway, the Children's Bureau, and FRIENDS National Resource Center for Community-Based Child Abuse Prevention. (2019). *2019 prevention resource guide.* Retrieved from https://www.childwelfare.gov/pubPDFs/guide_2019.pdf

Cole, S. F., Eisner, A., Gregory, M., & Ristuccia, J. (2013). *Helping traumatized children learn, volume 2: Creating and advocating trauma-sensitive schools.* Boston, MA: Massachusetts Advocates for Children.

Cole, S. F., Eisner, A., Gregory, M., & Ristuccia, J. (2019). *How can educators create safe and supportive school cultures?* Boston, MA: Massachusetts Advocates for Children. Retrieved from https://traumasensitiveschools.org/

Cole, S. F., O'Brien, J. G., Gadd, M. G., Ristuccia, J., Wallace, D. L., & Gregory, M. (2005). *Helping traumatized children learn: Supportive school environments for children traumatized by family violence.* Boston, MA: Massachusetts Advocates for Children.

Collaborative for Academic, Social, and Emotional Learning. (2019). Retrieved from https://casel.org/what-is-sel/

Council of State Governments Justice Center. (2011). *Breaking schools' rules: A statewide study of how school discipline relates to students' success and juvenile justice involvement.* New York, NY: Author. Retrieved from https://csgjusticecenter.org/wp-content/uploads/2012/08/Breaking_Schools_Rules_Report_Final.pdf

Cozolino, L. (2013). *The social neuroscience of education: Optimizing attachment & learning in the classroom.* New York, NY: W.W. Norton & Company.

Cozolino, L. (2014). *Attachment-based teaching: Creating a tribal classroom.* New York, NY: W.W. Norton & Company.

Craig, S. E. (1992). The educational needs of children living with violence. *Phi Delta Kappan, 74*(1), 67–68, 70–71.

Craig, S. E. (2017). *Trauma-sensitive schools for the adolescent years: Promoting resiliency and healing, grades 6–12.* New York, NY: Teachers College Press.

Cuellar, A. E., & Markowitz, S. (2015). School suspension and the school-to-prison pipeline. *International Review of Law and Economics, 43*, 98–106.

Dornfield, A. (2017, October 18). District didn't want us to visit this struggling Seattle school. *National Public Radio.* Retrieved from https://kuow.org/stories/district-didnt-want-us-visit-struggling-seattle-school/

Dube, S. R., Fairweather, D., Pearson, W. S., Felitti, V. J., Anda, R. F., & Croft, J. B. (2009). Cumulative childhood stress and autoimmune diseases in adults. *Psychosomatic Medicine, 71*(2), 243–250. doi:10.1097/psy.0b013e3181907888

Durlak, J. A., Dymnicki, A. B., Taylor, R. D., Weissberg, R. P., & Schellinger, K. B. (2011). The impact of enhancing students' social and emotional learning: A meta-analysis of school-based universal interventions. *Child Development, 82*(1), 405–432.

Echo. (2017a). *Dos and don'ts of a trauma-informed classroom.* Los Angeles, CA: Author. Retrieved from https://www.echotraining.org/resources

Echo. (2017b). *Trauma informed arrow.* Los Angeles, CA: Author. Retrieved from https://www.echoparenting.org/resources

Echo. (2017c). *"What do I do?": Trauma-informed support for children.* Los Angeles, CA: Author. Retrieved from https://www.echoparenting.org/resources

Echo. (2018). *You can't be trauma-informed if you can't see the trauma.* Retrieved from https://www.echotraining.org/you-cant-be-trauma-informed-if-you-cant-see-the-trauma/

Edwards, V. J., Dube, S. R., Felitti, V. J., & Anda, R. F. (2007). It's OK to ask about past abuse. *American Psychologist, 62,* 327–328. doi:10.1037/0003-066X62.4.327

Esrick, M. (Director). (2018). *Cracked up* [Motion picture]. United States: Ripple Effect Films.

Evans, K., & Vaandering, D. (2016). *The little book of restorative justice in education: Fostering responsibility, healing, and hope in schools.* New York, NY: Good Books.

Felitti, V. J., Anda, R. F., Nordenberg, D., Williamson, D. F., Spitz, A. M., Edwards, V., ... Marks, J. S. (1998). Relationship of childhood abuse and household dysfunction to many of the leading causes of death in adults: The Adverse Childhood Experiences (ACE) Study. *American Journal of Preventive Medicine, 14,* 245–258. doi:10.1016/S0749-3797(98)00017-8

Finkelhor, D. (2009). The prevention of childhood sexual abuse. *The Future of Children, 19*(2), 169–194. doi:10.1353/foc.0.0035

Fredrickson, B. L., Cohn, M. A., Coffey, K. A., Pek, J., & Finkel, S. M. (2008). Open hearts build lives: Positive emotions, induced through loving-kindness meditation, build consequential personal resources. *Journal of Personality and Social Psychology, 95*(5), 1045–1062.

Garner, A. S., Shonkoff, J. P., Siegel, B. S., Dobbins, M. I., Earls, M. F., McGuinn, L., ... Wood, D. L. (2012). Early childhood adversity, toxic stress, and the role of the pediatrician: Translating developmental science into lifelong health. *Pediatrics, 129*(1), 224–231. doi:10.1542/peds.2011-2662

Gonzalez, T., Etow, A., De La Vega, C., & Cribb-Fabersunne, C. (2018). The unintended consequences of school safety. *Education Week, 38*(13), 26–27.

Hammond, Z. (2015). *Culturally responsive teaching and the brain: Promoting authentic engagement and rigor among culturally and linguistically diverse students.* Thousand Oaks, CA: Corwin.

Hawn Foundation. (2011). *The mindup curriculum: Grades 6–8: Brain-focused strategies for learning and living.* New York, NY: Scholastic, Inc.

Hebb, D. O. (1949). *The organization of behavior.* New York, NY: Wiley.

Heitzeg, N. A. (2009). *Education or incarceration: Zero tolerance policies and the school to prison pipeline.* Forum on Public Policy. Retrieved from https://files.eric.ed.gov/fulltext/EJ870076.pdf

Hodas, G. (2006). *Responding to childhood trauma: The promise and practice of trauma-informed care.* Retrieved from http://www.childrescuebill.org/VictimsOfAbuse/RespondingHodas.pdf

Howes, C., & Ritchie, S. (2002). *A matter of trust: Connecting teachers and learners in the early childhood classroom.* New York, NY: Teachers College Press.

Hughes, K., Bellis, M. A., Hardcastle, K. A., Sethi, D., Butchart, A., Mikton, C., ... Dunne, M. P. (2017). The effect of multiple adverse childhood experiences on health: A systematic review and meta-analysis. *Lancet Public Health, 2*(8), e356–e366. doi:10.1016/S2468-2667(17)30118-4

Hughes, M., & Tucker, W. (2018). Poverty as an adverse childhood experience. *North Carolina Medical Journal, 79*(2), 124–126. doi:10.18043/ncm.79.2.124

Izumi, L. T. (2002). *They have overcome: High-poverty, high-performing schools in California.* San Francisco, CA: Pacific Research Institute. Retrieved from https://eric.ed.gov/?id=ED469963

Jensen, E. (2009). *Teaching with poverty in mind: What being poor does to kids' brains and what schools can do about it.* Alexandria, VA: ASCD.

Johnson-Reid, M., Drake, B., & Kohl, P. L. (2009). Is the overrepresentation of the poor child in welfare caseloads due to bias or need? *Children and Youth Services Review, 31,* 422–427. doi:10.1016/j.childyouth.2008.09.009

Justice Policy Institute. (2018). *Smart, safe, and fair: Strategies to prevent youth violence, heal victims of crime, and reduce racial inequality.* Washington, DC: Author. Retrieved from http://www.justicepolicy.org/research/12222

Karr-Morse, R., & Wiley, M. S. (2013). *Ghosts from the nursery: Tracing the roots of violence* (Rev. ed.). New York: NY: Atlantic Monthly Press.

Kendall-Tackett, K. A., & Eckenrode, J. (1996). The effects of neglect on academic achievement and disciplinary problems: A developmental perspective. *Child Abuse & Neglect, 20,* 161–169. doi:10.1016/S0145-2134(95)00139-5

Larkin, H., Felitti, V. J., & Anda, R. F. (2014). Social work and adverse childhood experiences research: Implications for practice and health policy. *Social Work in Public Health, 29,* 1–16. doi:10.1080/19371918.2011.619433

Larkin, H., & Records, J. (2007). Adverse childhood experiences: Overview, response strategy, and integral theory. *The Journal of Integral Theory & Practice, 2*(3), 1–25. Retrieved from http://www.aceresponse.org/img/uploads/file/Handouts2.pdf

Main, M., & Hesse, E. (1990). Parents' unresolved traumatic experiences are related to infant disorganized attachment status: Is frightened and/or frightening parental behavior the linking mechanism? In M. T. Greenberg, D. Cicchetti, & E. M. Cummings (Eds.), *Attachment in the preschool years: Theory, research, and intervention.* Chicago, IL: University of Chicago Press.

Maslow, A. H. (1943). A theory of human motivation. *Psychological Review, 50,* 370–396. doi:10.1037/h0054346

McEwen, B. S., Eiland, L., Hunter, R. G., & Miller, M. M. (2012). Stress and anxiety: Structural plasticity and epigenetic regulation as a consequence of stress. *Neuropharmacology, 62,* 3–12. doi:10.1016/j.neuropharm.2011.07.014

McEwen, B. S., & Gianaros, P. J. (2010). Central role of the brain in stress and adaptation: Links to socioeconomic status, health, and disease. *Annals of the New York Academy of Sciences, 1186,* 190–222. doi:10.1111/j.1749-6632.2009.05331.x

Meyer, L. H., & Evans, I. M. (2012). *The school leader's guide to restorative discipline.* Thousand Oaks, CA: Corwin.

National Child Traumatic Stress Network. (2008). *Child trauma toolkit for educators.* Retrieved from https://wmich.edu/sites/default/files/attachments/u57/2013/child-trauma-toolkit.pdf

National Child Traumatic Stress Network, Schools Committee. (2017). *Creating, supporting, and sustaining trauma-informed schools: A system framework.* Los Angeles, CA, and Durham, NC: National Center for Child Traumatic Stress. Retrieved from https://www.nctsn.org/resources/creating-supporting-and-sustaining-trauma-informed-schools-system-framework

National Institute for the Clinical Application of Behavioral Medicine (2017). *Guilt vs. Shame.* Storrs, CT: Author. Retrieved from https://www.nicabm.com/guilt-vs-shame/

National Scientific Council on the Developing Child. (2004). *Young children develop in an environment of relationships: Working Paper no. 1.* Cambridge, MA: Center on the Developing Child, Harvard University. Retrieved from https://developingchild.harvard.edu/resources/wp1/

Nelsen, J., Lott, L., & Glenn, H. S. (2000). *Positive discipline in the classroom: Developing mutual respect, cooperation, and responsibility in your classroom.* New York, NY: Three Rivers Press.

Nhat Hanh, T. (2009). *Happiness: Essential Mindfulness Practices.* Berkeley, CA: Parallax Press.

Norcross, J. C., & Barnett, J. E. (2008, Spring). Self-care as ethical imperative. *The Register Report,* pp. 20–27.

Nuri-Robins, K. J., Lindsey D. B., Lindsey, R. B., & Terrell, R. D. (2012). *Culturally proficient instruction: A guide for people who teach.* Thousand Oaks, CA: Corwin Press.

Oehlberg, B. (2008). Why schools need to be trauma informed. *Trauma and Loss: Research and Interventions, 8*(2), 1–4. Retrieved from http://www.traumainformedcareproject.org/resources/WhySchoolsNeedToBeTraumaInformed(2).pdf

Olson, K. (2014). *The invisible classroom: Relationships, neuroscience & mindfulness in school.* New York, NY: W.W. Norton & Company.

Perry, B. D. (1997). Incubated in terror: Neurodevelopmental factors in the "cycle of violence." In J. Osofsky (Ed.), *Children, youth and violence: The search for solutions* (pp. 124–148). New York, NY: Guilford Press.

Perry, B. D. (2000). Traumatized children: How childhood trauma influences brain development. *Journal of the California Alliance for the Mentally Ill, 11*(1), 48–51. Retrieved from https://www.aaets.org/article196.htm

Perry, B. D. (2001). The neurodevelopmental impact of violence in childhood. In D. Schetky & E. P. Benedek (Eds.), *Textbook of child and adolescent forensic psychiatry* (pp. 221–238). Washington, DC: American Psychiatric Press.

Perry, B. D. (2006a). Applying principles of neurodevelopment to clinical work with maltreated and traumatized children: The neurosequential model of therapeutics. In N. B. Webb (Ed.), *Social work practice with children and families: Working with traumatized youth in child welfare* (pp. 27–52). New York, NY: Guilford Press.

Perry, B. C. (2006b). *The boy who was raised as a dog: And other stories from a child psychiatrist's notebook.* New York, NY: Basic Books.

Perry, B. D. (2009). Examining child maltreatment through a neurodevelopmental lens: Clinical applications of the neurosequential model of therapeutics. *Journal of Loss and Trauma, 14,* 240–255. doi:10.1080/15325020903004350

Perry, B. D., & Pollard, R. (1998). Homeostasis, stress, trauma, and adaptation: A neurodevelopmental view of child trauma. *Child and Adolescent Psychiatric Clinics of North America, 7*(1), 33–51. doi:10.1016/s1056-4993(18)30258-x

Pritzker, K., & Scully, R. K. (Producers), & Redford, J. (Director). (2015). *Paper tigers* [Motion picture]. United States: KPJR Films.

Rak, C. F., & Patterson, L. E. (1996). Promoting resilience in at-risk children. *Journal of Counseling & Development, 74*(4), 368. https://doi.org/10.1002/j.1556-6676.1996.tb01881.x

Randall, T. (2019, January 4). Trauma informed care in a school setting. STARR Commonwealth. Retrieved from https://starr.org/trauma-informed-care-in-a-school-setting/

Roeser, R. W., Skinner, E., Beers, J., & Jennings, P. A. (2018). Mindfulness training and teachers' professional development: An emerging area of research and practice. *Child Development Perspectives, 6*(2), 167–173. Retrieved from https://www.pdx.edu/sites/www.pdx.edu.psy/files/Roeser,%20Skinner,%20Beers,%20&%20Jennings_Mindfulness_CDP_2012_Proofs.pdf

Romano, E., Babchishin, L., Marquis, R., & Frechette, S. (2015). Childhood maltreatment and educational outcomes. *Trauma, Violence, and Abuse, 16,* 418–437. doi:10.1177/1524838014537908

Romero, V. E., Robertson, R., & Warner, A. (2018). *Building resilience in students impacted by adverse childhood experiences: A whole-staff approach.* Thousand Oaks, CA: Corwin.

Schore, J. R., & Schore, A. N. (2008). Modern attachment theory: The central role of affect regulation in development and treatment. *Clinical Social Work Journal, 36*(1), 9–20.

Siegel, D. J. (2015). *Brainstorm: The power and purpose of the teenage brain.* New York, NY: Jeremy P. Tarcher/Penguin.

Siegel, D. J., & Bryson, T. P. (2010). *Mindsight: The new science of personal transformation.* New York, NY: Bantam Books.

Siegel, D. J., & Bryson, T. P. (2011). *The whole-brain child: 12 revolutionary strategies to nurture your child's developing mind.* New York, NY: Bantam Books.

Siegel, D. J., & Hartzell, M. (2014). *Parenting from the inside out: How a deeper self-understanding can help you raise children who thrive* (10th anniversary ed.). New York, NY: Jeremy P. Tarcher/Penguin.

Slopen, N., Shonkoff, J. P., Albert, M. A., Yoshikawa, H., Stoltz, R., & Williams, D. R. (2016). Racial disparities in child adversity in the United States: Interactions with family immigration history and income. *American Journal of Preventive Medicine, 50,* 47–56. doi:10.1016/j.amepre.2015.06.013

Smith, R., & Lambert, M. (2008). Assuming the best. *Educational Leadership, 66*(1), 16–21. Retrieved from http://www.ascd.org/publications/educational-leadership/sept08/vol66/num01/Assuming-the-Best.aspx

Souers, K., & Hall, P. (2019). *Relationship, responsibility, and regulation: Trauma-invested practices for fostering resilient learners.* Alexandria, VA: ASCD.

Spangler, G., & Grossman, K. E. (1993). Biobehavioral organization in securely and insecurely attached infants. *Child Development, 64*(5), 1439–1450. doi:10.2307/1131544

Spinazzola, J., Habib, M., Blaustein, M., Knoverek, A., Kisiel, C., Stolbach, B., ... Maze, J. (2017). *What is complex trauma? A resource guide for youth and those who care about them.* Los Angeles, CA, and Durham, NC: National Center for Child Traumatic Stress.

Sporleder, J., & Forbes, H. T. (2016). *The trauma-informed school: A step-by-step implementation guide for administrators and school personnel.* Boulder, CO: Beyond Consequences Institute.

Sroufe, L. A. (2005). Attachment and development: A prospective, longitudinal study from birth to adulthood. *Attachment & Human Development, 7,* 349–367. doi:10.1080/14616730500365928

Starr Commonwealth. (2019). *Trauma-informed care in a school setting.* Retrieved from https://starr.org/trauma-informed-care-in-a-school-setting/

Stevens, J. E. (2012, April 23). Lincoln High School in Walla Walla, WA, tries new approach to school discipline—suspensions drop 85%. *Aces Too High News.* Retrieved from https://acestoohigh.com/2012/04/23/lincoln-high-school-in-walla-walla-wa-tries-new-approach-to-school-discipline-expulsions-drop-85/

Streeck-Fischer, A., & van der Kolk, B. A. (2000). Down will come baby, cradle and all: Diagnostic and therapeutic implications of chronic trauma on child development. *Australian and New Zealand Journal of Psychiatry, 34,* 903–918. doi:10.1080/000486700265

Substance Abuse and Mental Health Services Administration. (2014). *SAMHSA's concept of trauma and guidance for a trauma-informed approach* (HHS Publication No. SMA 14-4884). Rockville, MD: Author. Retrieved from https://store.samhsa.gov/system/files/sma14-4884.pdf

Substance Abuse and Mental Health Services Administration—HRSA Center for Integrated Health Solutions. (n.d.). *Trauma.* Washington, DC: Author. Retrieved from https://www.integration.samhsa.gov/clinical-practice/trauma

Teicher, M. H., Samson, J. A., Anderson, C. M., & Ohashi, K. (2016). The effects of childhood maltreatment on brain structure, function and connectivity. *Nature Reviews: Neuroscience, 17,* 652–666. doi:10.1038/nrn.2016.111

Tyler, S., Allison, K., & Winslor, A. (2006). Child neglect: Developmental consequence, interventions and policy implications. *Child and Youth Care Forum, 35*(1), 1–20.

Udesky, L. (2018, June 11). Middle school tackles everybody's trauma; Result is calmer, happier kids, teachers and big drop in suspensions. *Aces Too High.* Retrieved from https://acestoohigh.com/2018/06/11/middle-school-tackles-everybodys-trauma-result-is-calmer-happier-kids-teachers-and-big-drop-in-suspensions/

Ulrich-Lai, Y. M., & Herman, J. P. (2009). Neural regulation of endocrine and autonomic stress responses. *Nature Reviews: Neuroscience, 10*(6), 397–409. doi:10.1038/nrn2647 van der Kolk, B. A. (2014). *The body keeps the score: Brain, mind, and body in the healing of trauma.* New York, NY: Viking.

van der Kolk, B. (2015, October 29). *Keynote address: "The body keeps the score."* Conference on the Advances in the Treatment of Eating Disorders: Integrating Research with Clinical Practice. Waltham, MA: Bentley College, Walden Center for Education and Research.

Walkley, M., & Cox, T. L. (2013). Building trauma-informed schools and communities. *Children & Schools 35*(2), 123–126.

Williams, M., & Penman, D. (2011). *Mindfulness: An eight-week plan for finding peace in a frantic world.* New York, NY: Rodale.

Wlodlowski, R. J. (1983). *Motivational opportunities for successful teaching.* Phoenix, AZ: Universal Dimensions.

Wolpow, R., Johnson, M. M., Hertel, R., & Kincaid, S. O. (2016). *The heart of learning and teaching: Compassion, resiliency, and academic success* (3rd ed.). Olympia, WA: Washington State Office of Superintendent of Public Instruction Compassionate Schools. Retrieved from http://www.k12.wa.us/compassionateschools/pubdocs/TheHeartofLearningandTeaching.pdf

Yerkes, R. M., & Dodson, J. D. (1908). The relation of strength of stimulus to rapidity of habit-formation. *Journal of Comparative and Neurological Psychology, 18,* 459–482. doi:10.1002/cne.920180503

Index

F

face-to-face communication, 25
family and community
    engagement, 126–127
fight, 20–21
flight, 20–21
four Ss of attachment, 34, 42, 116
freeze, 20–21
FRIENDS National Resource
    Center for Community-
    Based Child Abuse
    Prevention, 31

G

guessing game, 98
guilt, 44

H

Harris, Burke, 18
*Helping Traumatized Children
    Learn* (Cole), 76
hierarchy of needs (Maslow), 40,
    93–94
high school, 78–79
hippocampus, 20
household challenges, 57
hyperarousal behavior, 8
hypoarousal behavior, 8
Hypothalamic-Pituitary-Adrenal
    (HPA) Axis, 22
hypothalamus, 21

I

insecure attachment, 35–37
interpersonal trauma, 96
intervention, 97
inverted-U learning curve, 7

L

Lincoln High (school), Walla
    Walla, Washington, 4–5

M

Maslow, A. H., hierarchy of needs,
    40, 93–94
meditation, 101–103
middle school, 78–79
mindful awareness, 101

mindfulness, 101–103
mirror neurons, 25–27, 82

N

National Child Traumatic Stress
    Network (NCTSN), 78
National Scientific Council
    on the Developing Child,
    22–23
neglect, 4, 45, 57, 63
    emotional, 57
    physical, 58
neuroplasticity, 24–27
    mirror neurons, 25–27, 82
neuroscience, 5, 61
non-trauma-informed, 2, 11, 13
nonverbal communication, 25, 34,
    41, 81
nurturing, 10

O

occipital lobe, 21

P

Paper Tigers, 5
parental resilience, 127
parent communication, 126
Park Middle School in Antioch,
    California, 5
*Patterns of Attachment: A Psycho-
    logical Study of the Strange
    Situation* (Ainsworth), 32–33
Perry, B. D., 24, 26–27, 63, 74, 94,
    96–97, 104, 110, 117
power, of administrator, staff,
    teachers, 116–119
prefrontal cortex (PFC), 18
preschool, 78–79

R

reactive attachment, 37
regulated behavior, 8
relationship, 95–97
    interpersonal, 96
    nurturing, 96
    skills, 104
    teacher–student, 41–42
relationships skill, 83, 104
research, 62–63

resiliency, 98–99
responsive communication, 34
restorative discipline practices,
    120

S

safety, 74, 93–108
    emotional, 93–95
    physical, 93–95
school(s)
    attachment in, 38–50
    high, 78–79
    middle, 78–79
    trauma-informed, 1–14
school counselors, 76, 116–117
school staff power, 116–119
school to-prison pipeline, 2–3
schoolwide practices, 110–115
secure attachment, 33–35
self-awareness, 12, 43–44, 59, 104
self-care, 99–101
    strategies for, 100
self-management, 75–76, 104
self-regulation skills, 65, 127
shame, 44–46
skills
    cognitive, 41
    decision-making, 117, 121
    emotional, 41, 65
    relationship, 83, 104
    self-regulation, 18, 65, 127
    teaching, 103–104
social awareness, 104
social connections, 127
social-emotional competence of
    children, 127
social-emotional learning (SEL),
    103–104
social environments, 42–43
stigmatizing behavior, 80–83
strange situation, 32–33
stress response system, 22–24
    positive, 22–23
    tolerable, 22–23
    toxic, 23
    types of, 23
Substance Abuse and Mental
    Health Services
    Administration (SAMHSA), 6
support staff, 118–119
survival mode, 73

CPSIA information can be obtained
at www.ICGtesting.com
Printed in the USA
LVHW050900120123
736768LV00029B/424